EASTSI

cago Public Library

Reading is first : great ideas for teach

D1130408

CHICAGO PUBLIC LIBRARY
VODAK EASTSIDE BRANCH
3710 EAST 106 STREET
CHICAGO, IL 60617

ALSO BY GAYLE SKAGGS

On Display: 25 Themes to Promote Reading
(McFarland, 1999)

Off the Wall! School Year Bulletin Boards and Displays for the Library
(McFarland, 1995)

Bulletin Boards and Displays: Good Ideas for Librarians and Teachers
(McFarland, 1993)

Reading Is First

Great Ideas for Teachers and Librarians

by Gayle Skaggs

Illustrated by ROBERT L. SKAGGS

McFarland & Company, Inc., Publishers

Jefferson, North Carolina, and London

Library of Congress Cataloguing-in-Publication Data

Skaggs, Gayle, 1952–
Reading is first : great ideas for teachers and librarians / by Gayle
Skaggs ; illustrated by Robert L. Skaggs.
p.   cm.
Includes index.

ISBN 0-7864-1576-2 (softcover : 60# alkaline paper)

1. Reading (Elementary)—United States.   2. Children—Books
and reading—United States.   I. Title.
LB1573.S59   2003   372.41—dc21   2002156435

British Library cataloguing data are available

©2003 Gayle Skaggs and Robert L. Skaggs. All rights reserved

*No part of this book may be reproduced or transmitted in any form
or by any means, electronic or mechanical, including photocopying
or recording, or by any information storage and retrieval system,
without permission in writing from the publisher.*

Cover image: India Jade Roseman, age 6 *(Photograph by Karl-Heinz Roseman)*

Manufactured in the United States of America

*McFarland & Company, Inc., Publishers
Box 611, Jefferson, North Carolina 28640
www.mcfarlandpub.com*

R0404324719

To our wonderful granddaughters,
Danielle and Devyn

Chicago Public Library
Vodak/East Side Branch
3710 E. 106th St.
Chicago, IL 60617

Table of Contents

Table of Contents

Introduction

Learning to read is a milestone in everyone's life. The ability to read is powerful. Much of a child's success in other subjects is related to the ability to read. When the skill is new to children it is especially exciting, and if it is carefully guided and reinforced, reading can become a lifelong passion.

This book is designed to present to a school or individual teacher twenty suggestions for themes to promote reading and reading programs to elementary children, primarily those who need lots of extra motivation. The themes have been chosen for their high appeal. The key is to encourage and motivate children to read more and thereby improve their skills through lots of practice.

These themes were primarily developed for use with the Reading Counts or Accelerated Reader programs, but they could easily be adapted for others. One of the biggest obstacles with these reading programs is the cost. After the program has been purchased, the necessary computer equipment installed, etc., there are usually very few funds left for promotion. The novelty of the program soon wears off for the children, and what is needed for the long haul is a promotion to maintain their interest in the program. The promotion must be easy to put together but cost next to nothing. It must keep the children motivated throughout the year to read.

This book offers ideas for twenty such promotions. Each theme includes suggestions for wall displays to chart reading progress, possible assemblies to correspond to the theme, related Internet sites to explore, rewards or incentives for specified stages of achievement, ways of coordinating the theme to other subject areas, patterns for making display items, *and* directions on how to do it all on a shoestring budget.

Please note that the Internet sites listed were current at the time of this publication, but they may no longer be available, as this medium is constantly changing and updating. The Internet is a fabulous tool to incorporate into your theme and to give your students the opportunity to constructively practice their surfing skills.

Use the ideas as presented, or better yet, personalize them to meet the needs of your school and your individual readers. Many of the ideas are so simple that you will find yourself saying, "I can do that!" Happy reading!

Getting Started

The very best and most effective promotions are those that have been designed with your particular students and reading program in mind from the beginning. What is really appealing to your students? Ask them. The themes presented here might be used as written or as a springboard for your own creativity. Take bits and pieces from several chapters and create something totally unique for your school. The plans could be for a year-long presentation or for only a few months.

A large budget is not necessary to promote a reading program. The most important aspect is to let your joy of reading shine through your displays. If the display is exciting to you, it will surely be exciting to your students!

Be elaborate or keep things simple depending upon your particular needs, but always keep display materials looking fresh, clean, colorful, and exciting.

Don't fret if you don't consider yourself to be artistic. Use an opaque projector and just enlarge the patterns included in each chapter. Use letter patterns or computer-generate the words needed for the displays. Consider laminating items to lengthen their lifespan. Use and reuse items year after year to create new displays. Be sure to also include some maintenance time in your plans because even the best displays need to be freshened up from time to time.

To build up excitement, begin the year of reading with a poster contest to promote your chosen theme. This type of promotion is very effective regardless of the theme you choose. The first question asked will be, "What do I get if I win?" so first decide on an appropriate prize or prizes. An example of a sought-after prize at my school for the winning posters in grades 1–3 and in grades 4–6 was a $20 gift certificate for our school book fair. As we hosted the book fair as a fundraiser, there was no out-of-budget expense. Food coupons from local restaurants or gift certificates also work well. You might even consider some free homework passes or extra recess passes. Or the winners might become assistant principals for the day, a prize that costs nothing but offers a lot: a fun day with no school work.

Decide on the rules for your poster contest and put them in writing. It is a good idea to explain the contest to the other faculty members first so that they will be able to help answer questions. It is also good to send a note of explanation home to parents. Parental support and encouragement are very desirable.

A visit to each class to explain the rules and to get the children excited will boost participation. It is a good idea to provide the paper for the posters (12" × 18" is large enough). In this way all the entries will be the same size, making it easier for you to display them, and no one will be left out of the contest for lack of supplies.

Set a due date and stick to it—and prepare yourself to be amazed at the wonderful creativity of your students.

Display all the entries for a while, but mat or frame the winners to use throughout the year. Some of the posters could be scanned into the computer and used to create some really cool bookmarks. What an ego boost for a child to have his or her artwork used for a bookmark design for the whole school! These might also be added to the school website advertising the school's commitment to reading.

So pick a theme and get started. It won't be long before you are receiving many compliments on your displays and your students will be enjoying a great year of reading.

Basketball

Basketball and reading go together very well. Basketball is a theme that appeals to most children. They are excited by the names of professional basketball teams and players and by their own school teams and mascots. Even the smallest school districts usually have a basketball team as a source of school pride and competition.

A short pep assembly is a great idea as you begin the year. To go with the theme, invite the high school varsity basketball team, the cheerleaders, their coach and the pep band to pump up school spirit and enthusiasm. The team could put on a short exhibition of free throw shooting, etc., but you should also allow time for some of the players to talk about their favorite books or mention their favorite authors. Try to include some of your students in activities such as a dribbling relay or ball passing relay. This is also a great time to review how the reading program works and to announce the "principal's challenge" of the year.

Hopefully your principal is a good sport and willing to do something rather outrageous if a high percentage of the children reach their reading goal. For this theme, if your principal is a male, consider asking him to dress up as a female cheerleader complete with makeup, wig, and clothes and then do a cheer from the roof of the school. Or you might dress your principal up as the school mascot for the day.

Create a wall display to chart the children's progress in the program. If there are a large number of classes participating (such as a school-wide program), why not make a wall chart for each grade?

Choose a highly visible and well supervised spot in a hallway, the library or even the cafeteria for your progress chart. Students will take pride in seeing their markers move along the display.

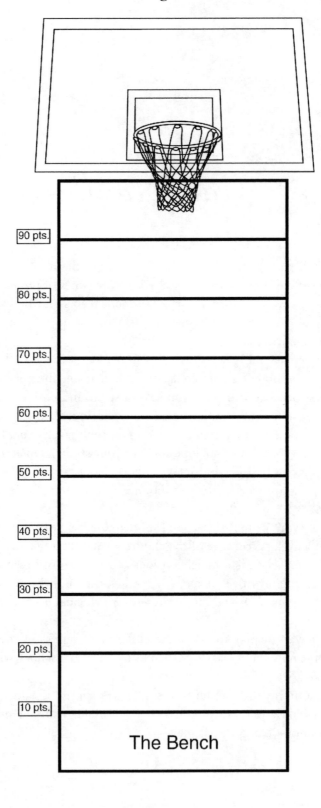

90 pts.

80 pts.

70 pts.

60 pts.

50 pts.

40 pts.

30 pts.

20 pts.

10 pts.

The Bench

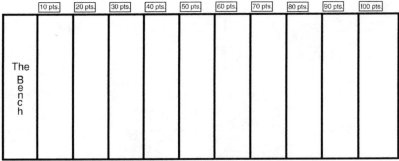

The chart could be horizontal or vertical. An easy method for creating a chart is to use painter's masking tape, which comes off the wall easily, leaving no residue. It is commonly available in a nice royal blue color.

Charts can also be made on large sheets of paper and hung on the wall. However, a paper background may be difficult to keep neatly on the wall for a whole school year. Moving children's markers along the chart also causes wear.

The computer-tested reading programs award points for each book read when correct answers are given to a series of ten questions. The children add the points throughout the year. If your reading program does not work in this way, consider counting the number of books read and use that as a basis to move the marker.

Our school goal is for each student to reach 100 points by the end of the year. We divide the chart into ten-point segments. The chart could be divided into any number of segments to fit your program. The overall size of the chart would be determined by the number of students you will be working with. Obviously more wall space is needed if you have many children in the program. The "Bench" area is always crowded at first because everyone begins at the same place. It won't be long before the markers will begin to be spaced throughout the chart.

If in your reading program each child has a different goal, consider using the painter's tape to mark off a basketball court as the basis for your wall chart. Half-court could be 50 percent of the goal with the remainder of the court divided up in areas such as 1–25 percent, 26–50 percent, etc. Be sure to include a bench area for everyone to have a place to begin with a marker.

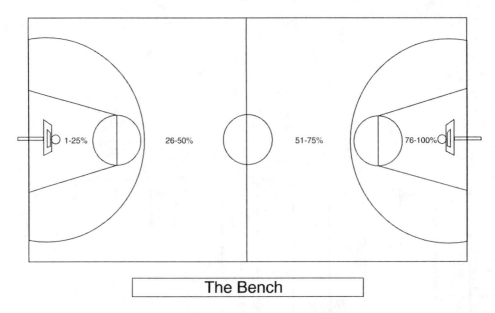

The Bench

This chapter contains three illustrations of possible charts: a vertical chart, a horizontal chart, and a chart using percentages of the goal earned. Any of these styles will get the job done.

You will need some type of basket on your wall chart. If you are making a vertical chart, the easiest thing to do is purchase an inexpensive basket such as one from a game set that comes with a foam ball. The hoops are plastic and have a white string net that easily fastens on. It usually has a heavy poster board backboard that the hoop snaps onto. The backboard that comes with this hoop may be too small for your wall chart. Consider replacing it with a piece of poster board and simply cut a hole in the poster board for the locking mechanism of the hoop.

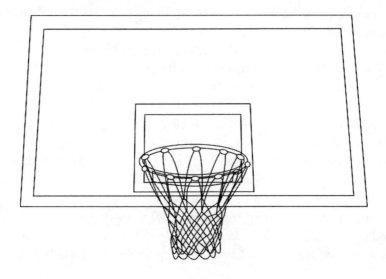

Tape it in place from the back. This whole thing can then be placed at the top of your wall chart, and it does give the display a realistic look.

If you can't find one of the plastic hoops, use a coat hanger and bend it into a circle. Before you fasten the ends together, slide on a piece of an old net. This could be an old basketball net (or a piece of an old white fish net). Then bend the ends of the wire together and put them through a small hole in a piece of poster board. Tape the ends down to keep the hoop in position.

If you prefer a two-dimensional net, use an opaque projector and enlarge the "Front-view basket/backboard" design. Use an orange marker to color in the rim of the basket. Laminate the backboard and rim and leave extra laminating film hanging down in the front. Use a black permanent marker to draw in the strings on that extra laminating film. Cut away the excess film to leave a neat basket. If you would like it to look more like a net, cut out some of the spaces between the strings.

Try a three-quarter view of the basket. The same procedure as described previously would work for this type of basket. Be sure to leave extra laminating film for a place to draw in the net for the basket. If you are really daring, make the backboard and rim out of poster board and add some real netting. It could be stapled on or taped from the back. Either way, it would look great!

Each child has a basketball to use as a marker. Included in this chapter is a basketball marker pattern. Copy it on orange or light brown construction paper and then laminate. Use a permanent black marker to add the child's name. If you do not want to have the child's name on the marker, use a classroom number system such as A3-1 (Adams 3rd grade—student 1). As the child earns points, the basketball is moved up, or across, toward the basket hoop. Have the child move his or her own marker once a week.

Each ten points earned means a prize for the child. It might be a pencil, an extra juice, a soda, or even the opportunity to skip one homework assignment. The prizes need not be costly—an extra recess is always a great prize and costs no money. Some students even consider it a prize to be allowed to help another teacher for part of the day or to have extra time in the library to read.

Another aspect of the display might be a scoreboard. List the teachers of a particular grade on a piece of poster board and add some bright stickers to look like marquee lighting. When a child earns 100 points, a mark is made on the scoreboard for the appropriate class. A gold star is added to the child's basketball

and the child begins again or the basketball is left in the net and a new basketball is added for the child. It could be interesting to see how many basketballs
a child might earn by the end of the year. Highly motivated readers may earn
1,000 points or more.

About halfway through the year, rekindle enthusiasm with a small contest.
Put all the names of students who have earned 100 points or more into a drawing. (Put their names in twice for 200 points, etc.) A basketball would be terrific
prize for the winner. Consider one for grades 1–3 and one for grades 4–6, or if
you have the funds, one for each grade.

Another way to boost enthusiasm would be to have each class create a poster
board team jersey. An example of one is provided in this chapter. The class could
choose a team name and a reading slogan with an appropriate graphic design.
These cost almost nothing and could really add some color and fun to the display. Laminate them if possible to lengthen their life, as you will want them to
last throughout the year. These could be hung from the ceiling or placed on the
wall near the progress chart. You could have a ceremony at the end of the year
to retire the jerseys and celebrate a fantastic year of reading.

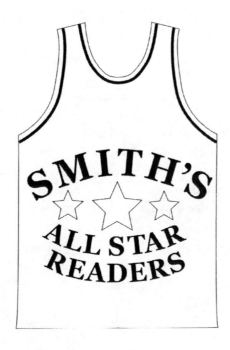

Brainstorm for all the basketball-reading slogans you can come up with.
Here are some to consider:

Hoop-It-Up with Reading!

Score Big ... READ!
Slam ... Dunk ... Read!

Purchase posters of famous basketball players reading. These are readily available in poster and school supply catalogs or on the Internet. Consider taking pictures of some of your own school district's high school basketball stars reading to serve as role models for your students. Check your school library for biographies of players to feature. Encourage your students to write to some of these players and find out about their favorite books (some may even send autographed pictures, which could become valuable prizes!). Letter writing is a skill all students need to practice. Some athletes and most professional teams have websites your students could explore. These are a few possible sites to check out:

- www.nba.com—The official website of the National Basketball Association. This site has links to all 29 national teams.

- www.WNBA.com—Women's National Basketball Association.

- www.hoophall.com—Naismith Memorial Basketball Hall of Fame.

Spend some time learning the rules of basketball. A class discussion could be held on the importance or significance of rules. Why do we have them? Who makes the rules? Talk about good sportsmanship and fair play with your students. What does teamwork mean? How can skills learned in playing this game prepare a person for the working world and life in general?

For a math activity, have your students calculate their points, subtract to find the number they still need to earn, or compute the fractional value. Find the circumference of a basketball and do comparisons to other spheres such as the earth.

For spelling, practice on basketball related words such as:

basketball	court	league
referee	dunk	defense
player	team	backboard
point	forward	opponent
guard	rim	score
slam	foul	hoop
dribble	pass	shoot

Don't forget about parents, and consider involving the PTA or PTO. Organize a basketball game between the parents and the students or the teachers and the students or a combination. Consider a "donkey" ball game. Those are always

I've scored 100 points in Reading

I've scored 100 points in Reading

I've scored 100 points in Reading

I've scored 100 points in Reading

a big hit and are probably available in your area. Invite some of the local leaders to come and play a game, such as your mayor, police chief, firemen, your local television weatherman, etc. People will get involved when they understand that you are promoting reading and doing something special for the children of your community. This type of ball game is usually a great fundraiser and funds collected could be used to purchase more library books or needed classroom supplies.

Children like bookmarks and their use does help to protect book pages. Copy the designs provided or create one of your own on tag board or heavy construction paper. Laminate if possible. This is a very inexpensive way to keep the year's reading theme in front of everyone. For a little extra pizazz, punch a hole and add yarn or ribbon.

These ideas are just the tip of the iceberg. Try some of them and enjoy yourself this year as your students improve their reading skills and have the best year of reading ever.

Baseball

The great American pastime would serve well to spark a productive year of reading. The usual nine months of a school year correspond to the nine innings of a baseball game. Your classroom teachers are the best coaches and your principal would be similar to the Commissioner of Baseball. So, batter (reader) up!

Does your high school have a baseball team? Have a big opening assembly featuring these players. Allow time for them to mention their favorite book or author and encourage their coach to say a few words about the importance of reading in his or her life. Do some simple relays with the children to get everyone involved. Don't forget to invite the high school pep band to add some spark to the festivities. "Take Me Out to the Ball Game" would be a perfect song to feature.

Encourage the children to all wear their summer ball team shirts to this opening assembly. Rent or borrow a large popcorn machine and set up a popcorn stand for everyone to grab a small bag on their way out of the assembly.

Supply baseball caps for the faculty with some baseball related slogans such as:

Become an All-Star Reader.
Be the Designated Reader!
Have You Gotten in Your Practice Time Today?
Homerun Reader!
Get in the Game … READ!

Using poster board, have each class create a team T-shirt. (A real shirt could even be used.) Make a simple pattern for these poster board shirts and then trace them all at one time. This will insure they are all uniform in size and shape. Distribute them to the classes to be personalized with a class team name and mascot or a reading related phrase. As the classes enter the opening assembly area, have each class proudly carry in their team shirt. Retire these at the end of the school year or the conclusion of this theme.

Decorate the halls with paper bats, gloves, and baseballs. Simple baseball diamonds with the word "READ" added could be hung around the halls. Hang posters of famous ball players; many are available that actually promote reading. Check your poster supply catalogs. The cafeteria staff may also have posters of baseball players drinking milk. These would support your theme and help to involve other areas of the school.

To chart reading progress, create a large baseball diamond on the wall. One would be needed for each grade, or a smaller version could be made for each classroom. Use any color of painter's tape to make the base lines. Be sure the tape you use does not remove the wall's paint. Use a permanent marker to mark off point or percentage designations on the painter's tape. Label these. Add a square of laminated construction paper for each base with the number or per-cent achieved written on it in permanent marker. For example: 25%, 50%, 75%, 100% or Home. A dugout area on each side of home plate provides a place for each child to begin. The child's baseball marker would stay in the dugout until points are earned or a number of books are read.

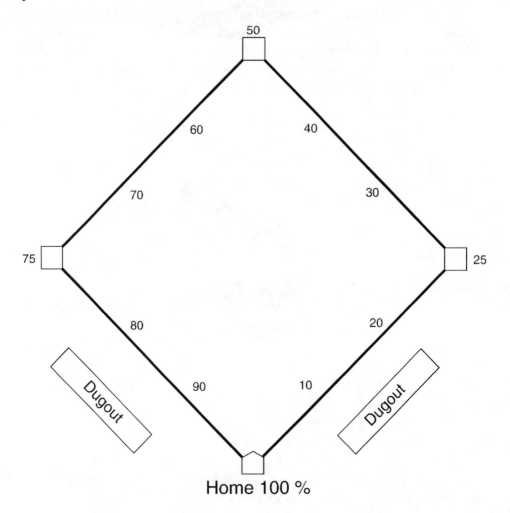

Create a scoreboard and laminate it. Put each classroom teacher's name on the scoreboard with a place to write in tally marks for each time a run, or 100 points, or some other benchmark is earned.

Display a large United States map with all the major league teams' home cities marked. Mark the leagues in different colors, such as the National League teams in blue and the American League in red. Make a display of the mascots.

The World Series is always played in October. Plan some special reading promotion during the series. For example, put all the names of the children who have earned 25 points in a specified period of time into a drawing for a prize such as a new ball glove, a ball and bat, a cool shirt, or the like. Check with your local sporting goods store and see if a discount might be possible or if they might

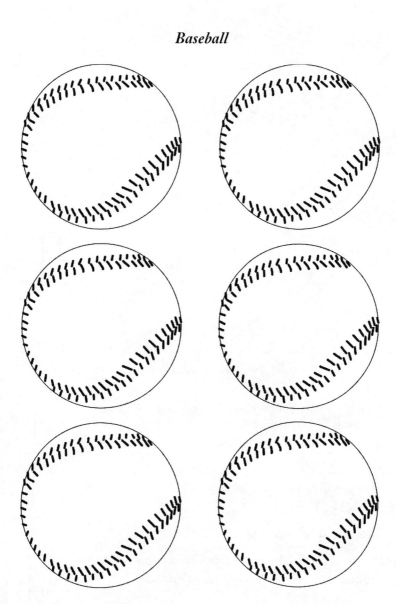

donate prizes. Ask your PTO or PTA for some assistance. Parents are really vital to a successful reading program.

The seventh inning stretch is always fun at the ball game. During the seventh month of school, plan a special activity to spur on those readers who are in a slump. Everyone who earns 25 points during this month could receive an extra thirty minutes of recess. This is a valuable prize and everyone has the same chance to receive it. The financial cost is nothing, but oh what a boost!

When the weather is good, host a faculty versus the sixth grade baseball game or a parents versus the older students ball game. The students who are eligible to play would be all those in a specified grade who have completed the reading goal set for the program. Form cheering sections and serve popcorn. This would be a great way to end the year of reading.

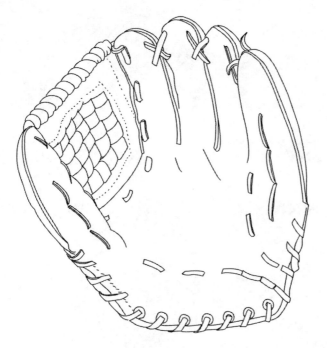

There are many cool websites to try out for baseball:

- http://www.mlb.com—This is the official site of Major League Baseball.

- http://www.baseballhalloffame.org—The National Baseball Hall of Fame.

- http://www.baseballamerica.com

- http://www.baseball-almanac.com—This is baseball history, awards, records, humor, feats, etc.

Possible spelling words to feature might be:

umpire	dugout	teamwork
coach	series	strike
pitcher	shortstop	foul
infield	catcher	offense
sportsmanship	league	inning

For math class, do problems to figure a player's batting average. Baseball math can also be done by creating on the chalkboard a home plate and three bases. Assemble two teams and start the game. Ask the first child on the team to answer a particular problem, whether addition, subtraction, multiplication or division. If the correct answer is given, the child moves to first base. Go on to the next child, and so on. An incorrect answer is an out. Three outs and the other team is up to the plate. Continue as time allows.

Football

Football is a very popular sport and one that just might grab the attention of some reluctant readers. Choose symbols and characteristics of football to point to reading. This could work in a similar way to the basketball theme. Many of the ideas listed there could be modified to fit this sport.

Begin the year with a pep assembly. If your school district has a high school football team, invite them to participate. Younger children look up to their high school heroes and would be interested to hear which authors and books these athletes like best. Ask them to put on a small exhibition. Be sure to include cheerleaders and make this a spirited event complete with the high school pep band and the school mascot.

A green tarp would make a great background for a football field to chart the children's reading progress. Paint on lines or use tape to designate points or percentages earned. Create footballs for chart markers by photocopying the pattern included in this chapter. Use light brown or orange construction paper. Laminate the footballs and write the children's names on them in permanent black marker.

Brainstorm for all the football related words you can think of to use as catchy slogans. Consider these:

Tackle a Good Book Today.
Punt, Pass and Read!
Pass on a Good Book to a Friend.
The Super Bowl of Reading!

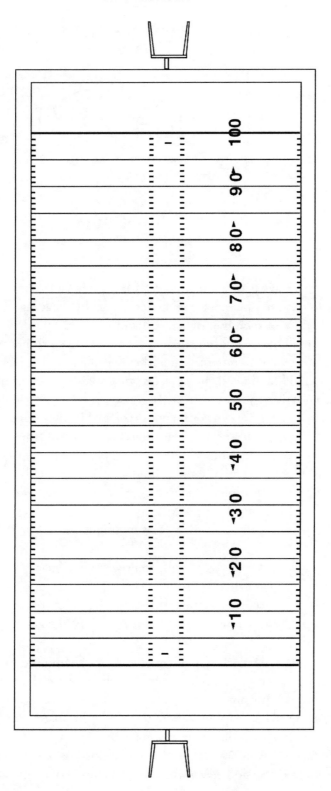

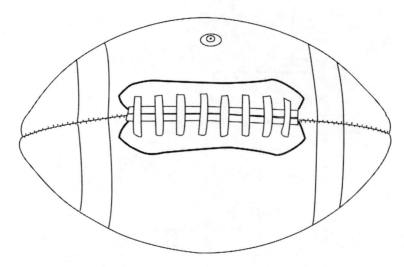

Many fans wave team pennants or spirit flags at football games. Challenge each class to design a pennant which ties football to reading. These could be made from fabric or merely poster board and fastened to a dowel rod or stick. These flags could be used in the opening assembly as a spirit booster. Each time a student reaches 100 points or some other specified goal, a ribbon or strip of crepe paper could be tied on the pennant stick. This could become quite a trophy by the end of the year.

Decorate the hallways in your school's colors. Hang up paper helmets, footballs, and goal posts, and set out some old school football trophies and pictures of your school mascot. Use the real items when possible in display cases or other display areas. Hang posters of famous football players actually reading or regular posters with conversation balloons added that contain encouraging comments about books and reading.

Some possible spelling words to feature might be:

tackle	defensive	guard
quarterback	halfback	safety
linebacker	helmet	goal
interference	referee	kicker

Create some bookmarks for this theme. Copy them onto bright cardstock or construction paper and then laminate. Punch a hole in the top and add ribbon or yarn to match your school colors.

Hang a large U.S. map on a prominent bulletin board. Put on small flags marking the home locations of professional football teams. A display of the many team mascots would look great, too. Use this as a way to teach a geography lesson. Get a discussion going with your students about why some cities have

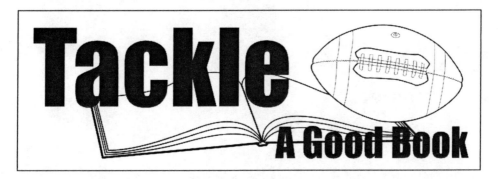

pro teams and some do not. When was the first Super Bowl? What two teams participated? Create some math problems based on the total scores, etc.

Try one of these websites:

- http://www.nfl.com—This is the official National Football League site.
- http://www.profootballhof.com—This is the ProFootball Hall of Fame site.

Soccer

Soccer is a tremendously popular sport for young people. It has actually been played longer in the United States than all our other major sports. This theme could be an exciting base for a great year of reading. Consider it for a year-long plan or for just a month or two.

Does your school have a soccer team? If so, ask the team to put on an exhibition to spark excitement for the beginning of this reading promotion. Ask several of the team members to share their favorite book or favorite author. Present the principal's reading challenge to the children and spend some time explaining how the program functions. Be ready to answer questions and all the "what ifs" that children like to ask. Encourage your principal to choose something really silly or bizarre as the challenge.

Each class should choose a team name and create a team jersey from poster board. These could all be hung together from the ceiling in the entry area of the school or by each individual classroom. Make a pattern for the shirt and cut out all the jerseys you need. This will insure that all of them will be the same shape and size. More teachers will be willing to participate if the shirt is already drawn and cut out.

To create a green soccer field for a wall chart, use a green tarp carefully taped or hung on the wall. Green paper would work but the paper's finish begins to

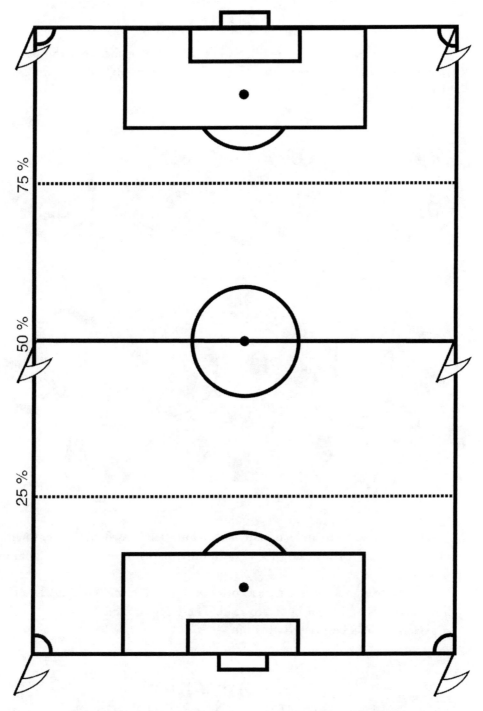

look a little tattered after the markers are moved several times. Use white tape to mark off the lines on the field. Add some flags to mark the corner boundaries. The plan will be to begin in the end-sideline area and move across the field to score a goal. The area can be divided up by points or percentages with the center line serving as 50 percent or 50 points.

Use soccer balls as chart markers that have been made from the pattern included in this chapter. Run white construction paper through the copy machine and then laminate it. Use a permanent red or blue marker to add the child's name.

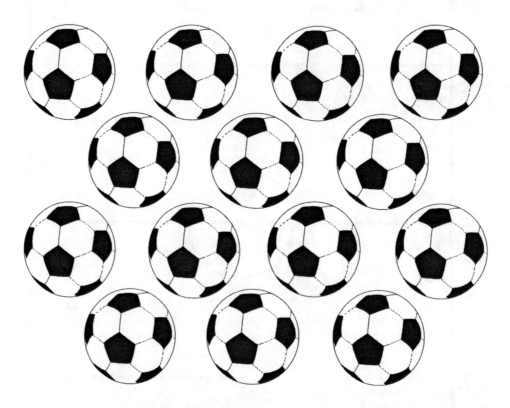

Create a scoreboard and laminate it also. Put each classroom teacher's name on the scoreboard with a place to write in tally marks for each time a goal of 100 points, etc. is scored.

Use a soccer goal net to create a cool reading area in the library. Add a few pillows and a cart of great books to read. These might include biographies of star players such as Pele or Mia Hamm.

Here are a few slogans to consider:

Books Are a Kick!
We Get a Kick Out of Reading!
Good Reading Is Our Goal!

Good sportsmanship is such an important lesson to teach. Try to pull from the game of soccer any opportunity to point out the value of honesty, hard work, and tenacity. Children need to learn to play by the rules and to play for fun.

Another valuable lesson is learning to work together as team members. In soccer, no player can win the game alone. Every player is important. Communication skills need to be developed for the game of soccer and for later in life. This is a great opportunity for some collaborative activities for your students to reach a common goal.

These might be some good spelling words to feature:

forward	penalty	midfielder
foul	defender	charging
goalkeeper	offside	kickoff
shinguard	passing	cleat

There are five basic soccer skills that every player needs to learn: kicking, passing, dribbling, heading, and trapping. Mastering these skills will help create a great soccer player. Tie these to the specific skills you want your students to master in math, language arts, and other subjects.

In math class, create some problems based on a standard soccer field size. What is the length and width of the field in yards, feet, and inches? What is the area of the field?

For younger students, work on the concept of time. Soccer games are often made up of two 45-minute halves. Practice telling time or just locating the second hand of the clock. How do a digital clock and a standard clock differ?

Soccer players must be physically fit. Much running is required for a considerable period of time. Lessons on good nutrition and the value of plenty of exercise could be taught in P.E. classes. Children always seem to love to do anything the "Coach" thinks is cool, so stress more physical activity. Sedentary lifestyles and excess weight are endangering the health of our children.

Because soccer is played in so many countries around the world, tie the game to a study of other nations. One of the most successful countries in World Cup play has been Brazil. Feature the Brazilian flag along with those of other soccer countries and hang them in a designated area of the hall or a corner of the cafeteria. Learn about these cultures and why soccer is so popular among their people. This is a great opportunity to add more multiculturalism to your curriculum.

Also, check out http://www.mlsnet.com, Major League Soccer's official site.

Racing to Read

Start your engines! The race to read is on! Race cars and racing have become a popular American pastime. This might just be the perfect theme to get your students on the road to a great year of reading.

Celebrate your "Pit Crew" by supplying T-shirts or caps printed with the theme's name or slogan. All of the teachers, your librarian, the school secretary, and especially the principal are the Pit Crew. The crew of a real racing team works to keep the driver going at all times. Your crew will be working to keep your students on track with their reading. The students will make "pit stops" at the library as they refuel with new books.

There are many great slogans that would be appropriate for this theme:

The Reading Derby
The Reading Speedway
The Race Is On
Reading in High Gear
All Geared Up for Reading
You "Auto" Be Reading
Stop … Think … Read!
Racing to Read

Create a race track for a wall chart to keep pace with the students' reading progress. The wall chart could be a circular track or a long horizontal track.

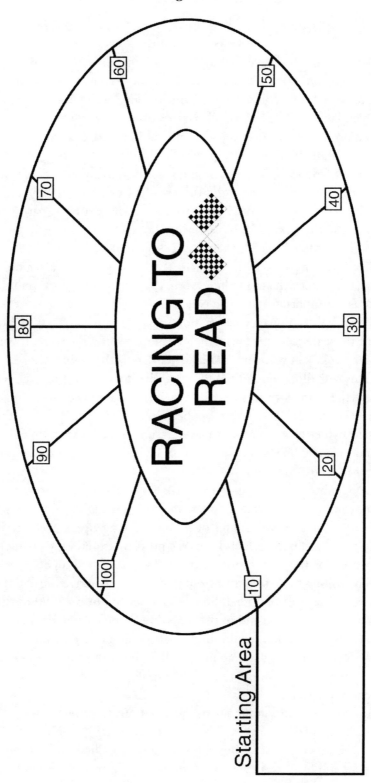

Heavy black plastic works well as the main material to construct either type of track.

For a circular track, cut out an oval from the black plastic and tape it to the wall, being sure that all edges are taped down. A considerable amount of space will be needed. Using colored tape, divide the area with point or percentage lines which you label. Add some small flags or other race-related graphics to finish off the track scene. A cheering section could be added at the top of the track using some light blue or white paper. Smiley-face stickers or a stamper could put cheerful, encouraging faces at the race. A starting area could be added to line up the cars at the beginning of the reading race.

A horizontal track would work well if you have a long, narrow wall space available. Use the heavy black plastic and be sure to tape it well. Divide up the area and label each space. A cheering section could be added to this also.

Black poster paper looks great in the beginning, but after moving a few markers, the paper will start to look worn. Plastic will be more durable and maintenance is an important factor to consider.

Run a light color of construction paper or card stock through the copy machine to create race cars for markers to move around the track. If you are using a circular track, you will need to make markers with the image of a car on both sides. This will allow you to keep the car facing forward as the track turns. Make copies of the pattern that is included in this chapter, cut out the car, and fold between the twin images. These can be colored and customized by the students with their names prominently displayed. Laminate the cars to increase their life span and to create one car with two good sides. For the horizontal track, a one-sided car is adequate.

An opening assembly to get everyone pumped up is a great way to begin the year. Encourage everyone to wear whatever "racing" clothing they have. Play some peppy music or the sound of motors revving up as everyone enters the assembly area. After introductions of the pit crew, explain the racing theme, the reading goal for the year and the principal's challenge. Hopefully your principal will be willing to do something outrageous to encourage the children to work hard toward their reading goal. Some examples might be: if 90 of the students achieve their goal by the end of the school year, the principal will be dunked in a dunk tank, the children could throw wet sponges or creme pies at him or her, or he or she might even dress up in a gorilla suit for the day. The sillier the challenge, the better. The humiliation of the principal lasts for only a short time but the benefits are great!

To add some entertainment to the assembly, have relay races. Make three or four race cars from cardboard boxes that have large openings in the top and bottom. Use several sizes of boxes—a small size for first and second grade and one big enough for your largest older student to fit over his or her head. Be sure

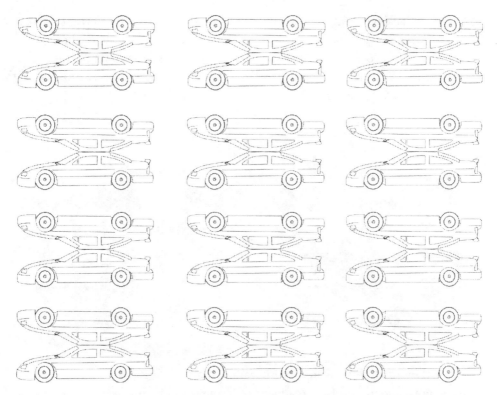

to plan for this difference in size, as the whole purpose of the assembly is to have fun and get everyone involved in the theme. Paint these boxes to look like cool little cars with cardboard circles for wheels and, of course, a fake steering wheel. Attach pieces of rope that can fit over the children's shoulders to hold the cars on as they race. Hold relays with the cars as time allows. These will be similar to Flintstone cars and should be fun to see as the children maneuver them around safety cones or other obstacles.

Use black and white checkered flags throughout the school. Wrapping paper or gift paper is available in this design and can be used for bulletin board backgrounds. Many local businesses display large or life-size cutouts of drivers. Ask if these items could be donated to the school when the store is finished with them, or check poster supply catalogs for possibilities.

Other road signs would work well for decorating. Use stoplights, speed limit signs, and all kinds of road signs. These could be made from poster board or simply created on the computer. They would also make great bookmark designs.

Colorful banners are great attention-getters. Try to use a racing related word like NASCAR to make a statement about reading. Use the letters to create a reading phrase such as:

N	Not
A	A
S	Surprise….
C	Children
A	Are
R	Reading!

If you have planned and promoted the reading theme, it won't be a surprise. Your students will be reading and reading and reading.

Check out these websites for idea inspiration or for your students to learn more about car racing: http://www.nascar.com; and http://www.autoracing.about.com.

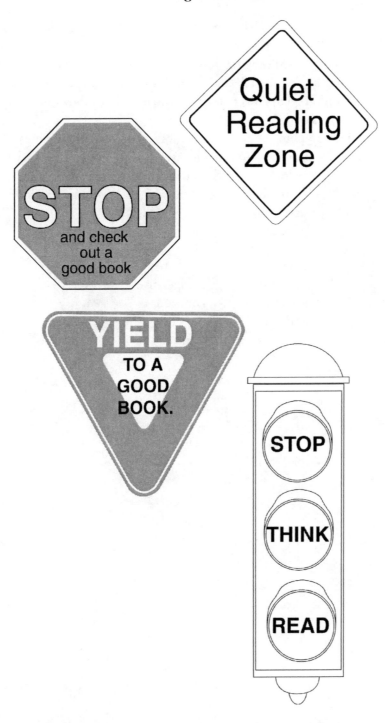

This theme would lend itself to discussions of safety. Stress automobile safety and bicycle safety. Check with your state department of transportation, the Highway Patrol, or even the health department for free handouts for your students. These websites are designed for kids: http://www.ottoclub.org; and http://www.kenkifer.com/bikepages/traffic/.

Math could be tied in with story problems using the names of real drivers. Problems could be created for calculating distance and speed in a race. Example: If Jeff Gordon completes one lap in three minutes, how many laps will he finish in thirty minutes?

The librarian could prepare an exhibit of drivers' biographies. A few old tires that have been cleaned up could be used to display these books, which could include current personalities in the racing world along with some of the old greats: Dale Earnhardt, Jeff Gordon, Richard Petty, Bobby Allison, A.J. Foyt, Mario Andretti, Rusty Wallace, or Davey Allison.

Spelling words for this theme might include:

racing	excitement	track
dangerous	competitive	speed
automobile	collision	noisy
speedway	driver	danger
helmet	caution	safety

Seeing the U.S.A.

We as Americans are so proud of our country; but, how much do we really know about it from coast-to-coast? We seem to fall short when asked geography questions. This theme could be exciting and educational for the children and the faculty. There is something for everyone as you travel across the nation via a year of reading. Most of your students have traveled at least a short distance from home and have some experience in seeing new places, but there are new things to learn about, places to pretend to go and people to meet. This could be like a giant field trip.

Begin your planning by creating a wall chart to record students' reading progress through the year. The wall chart is important because it helps to keep the children focused. Use a large U.S. map as the base or, using an opaque projector, create a simple wall-sized outline map. Divide the map into sections representing points or percentages depending upon your reading program. You will need to decide which way you want to move across the United States and put in the points or percentages accordingly. Draw in the section lines with a dark marker or use masking tape or colored plastic tape.

It might be interesting to begin on the East coast and move westward, the same way our country was settled. Beginning in New England in the fall would allow you to use lots of colorful leaves for decorations since fall foliage is a very big attraction in New England. The children could work toward a beach party on the West coast as an end of the year activity.

As the students move across the map of the U.S., they might create postcards to send to others in the school. For example, when a student earns ten points, he or she might create a postcard for a special location in the East or New England. This could be the Statue of Liberty, the Liberty Bell, a lighthouse or some other landmark. The cards could be done on tag board or cut from

35

poster board and colored with markers. If your school has an in-house mail system for students between classrooms, allow the cards to be sent through that mail system. They could also be hand-delivered to residents in a nursing home as a community outreach project for the school. Otherwise, you might just want to begin a large postcard display somewhere in the building.

Research the route you have chosen across the country and display interesting facts. The research could be done by one class throughout the year or the area could be divided among many classes. The school could even be divided up with areas designated as New England, the Midwest, and other regions. This could become a large, magnificent display with each area of the building decorated to represent a part of the country.

This theme could also be done in another time period. Consider going on the trail with Lewis and Clark or as pioneers moving across the nation. Covered wagons would make great markers. Feature books by Laura Ingalls Wilder and biographies of early pioneers. Host a dress-up day in the time period with appropriate food and games.

Another time period to consider might be the '50s with, of course, a sock hop as a reading incentive. Use vintage car designs for markers and possibly follow Route 66 across the U.S. Throw in a jukebox and black posterboard 45s to decorate. Your students may not know what a 45 record is! Invite grandparents to share personal experiences or to show some old home movies. Your school probably has a collection of old yearbooks that your students would love to look through. What did the homecoming queen of the 1950s wear to the dance? Use your wonderful community resources and get as many people involved as possible.

For a little different wall chart, use a physical map of the U.S. or make a simple outline map and have students paint in the rivers, mountains, and other features, as everything was for the time period you have chosen. Mark it off in ten point areas or by percentages. Each grade might make their own to promote more pride and ownership in the program.

There are many great possibilities for markers for the wall chart. Consider suitcases, covered wagons, footprints, tennis shoes, or school buses.

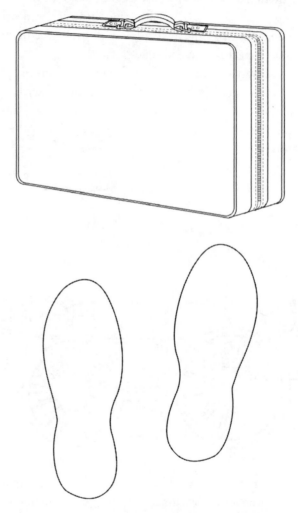

Other decorating ideas could include the state nicknames. "Show Me," Missouri's nickname, could be put on signs saying "Show Me" you can read. *The World Almanac* has all the state nicknames listed, in addition to the state birds, trees, flowers, and other symbols. Also listed is the tourism website for each state. An example is http://www.missouritourism.org. You could also try http://www.towd.com or http://www.statelocalgov.net/index.cfm.

Use lots of red, white and blue and be sure to feature the American flag prominently. This is a great opportunity to teach about citizenship and what is expected of an American citizen. It would be a very effective theme to use during an election year.

Display travel books in the library and consider using old suitcases to create display spaces. Vary the selection by constantly featuring different areas of our country. Have your students create travel posters or even travel-related bookmarks.

Use old maps of places in the U.S. to cut up for letters and bulletin board backgrounds. Distribute maps of your state to all the children and practice map skills. Teach the children how to use the grid method of locating a city, town, etc. In Missouri, maps are available from the Missouri Department of Transportation. (It is probably the same in other states.) Your state tourism department would know where to get free maps.

For math practice, figure the miles between two points or the number of miles traveled in a certain number of hours. Discuss the concept of time zones and practice using these.

Partner your class with another class elsewhere in the nation by becoming email pen pals, or correspond the old-fashioned way. Our students need more experience in writing and this would be a great way to get in that much-needed practice and have fun at the same time. Have your students pick a state they would like to correspond with and then check the official state website. Look for a listing of public school districts and contact some to check for interest in becoming pen pals. These are some additional U.S. pen pal email websites:

- http://www.epals.com
- http://www.siec.k12.in.us/~west/online/coll1a.htm
- http://www.iwaynet.net/~jwolve/school.html

Create puzzles relating to this theme to test student knowledge. Many puzzle programs are available on the 'net. This one will allow you to make word searches, crossword puzzles, mazes, cryptograms, number blocks, and hidden message word searches: http://www.puzzlemaker.com.

Through the year, try spelling words like:

travel	America	map
landmark	visit	highway
museum	tourist	sightseeing
suitcase	exploration	journey

For social studies, organize a competition among your older students on geography trivia. Ask the names of states and capitals, rivers, mountains, and other geographic features. Keep the prizes simple but offer a lot of praise.

For science, research all of the zoos across the United States. What are the most common animals kept in these zoos? How many zoos are there and where are they located? Why do we have zoos and what is involved in maintaining one? These websites might be helpful:

- http://www.zooweb.net
- http://aolsvc.travel.aol.com/travel/interest/safaris.jsp
- http://www.aza.org
- http://www.pbs.org

We see a map of the United States every night on the news when the weather report is given. How does the weather in one part of the country influence the weather in another area? Do an in-depth study of weather patterns and global warming, El Niño, tornadoes, or hurricanes. What is the safest part of the country to live in? Invite someone from the National Weather Service or a local television weatherman to visit the school and talk to your students.

Everyone has a favorite professional ball team of one kind or another. Display a large map showing every major league baseball team or football team. Both could be done since the season for each doesn't overlap too much. Where is the Super Bowl being held, or the World Series? Use sports to teach geography in any way that you possibly can.

Many schools have a map of the United States painted on their playground. This would be a great project for an art club or the PTA or PTO. This could serve as a fun meeting spot on the playground and would be available for many learning activities.

The possibilities for this theme are endless. What a great way to promote a year of reading and an opportunity to celebrate living in America!

Around the World in a School Year

Our world appears to get smaller and smaller now that we are all connected by the internet, yet we know so little about other parts of our world, especially those that haven't recently been on the nightly news. This theme offers so many wonderful multicultural opportunities for a school-wide celebration of great reading.

A great beginning display would be to hang a large world map on a very visible bulletin board. Using small flags or stickers, mark with names and dates the places outside the United States visited by faculty and staff members. The words "Where Have You Been?" would be appropriate for a display of this type.

Divide the school into continent areas: Asia, Europe, Africa, North America, South America, and Australia. Antarctica would be interesting, but could limit some of the activities you might want your class to do. You might also want to limit North America to Canada, Mexico and Central America, and save the United States for a whole theme by itself. (See the previous chapter.) Each classroom in these areas could choose a country to become during the year. They could focus on learning more about that particular country and share what they learn with the rest of the school throughout the year. This would not have to dominate the curriculum, but could be used just as a way to tie the year of reading together.

Each hallway could be decorated in flags from the countries of that continent. These flags can be made from construction paper, laminated, and hung from the hallway ceilings. They could be used end-to-end to create a cool border in the hall. *The World Almanac* features flags of the world for quick reference.

To continue the decorating theme, mark off appropriate areas as the equator, prime meridian, or other features of the globe. Organize student activities around these focal points. Anything we can use to help children with geography skills will be a big plus.

Sponsor a door-decorating contest which features the word "reading" in the particular country chosen. Some examples are La Lectura(Spanish), Legere (Latin), Das Lesen (German), and La Lecture (French). Check the foreign dictionaries of the library's reference section to get more words for reading.

To chart the students' reading progress, use a world map or enlarge one with an opaque projector to make it wall-sized. Divide this area into point segments or percentages using tape or draw in the lines with a dark marker. Many items would be great possibilities for the students' markers such as hot air balloons, airplanes, or suitcases (stickers could be added to the suitcase each time a goal has been met).

The students will need a folder to document their reading. Create these to look like passports. The front cover could say something like, "Passport to a great year of reading." The child's

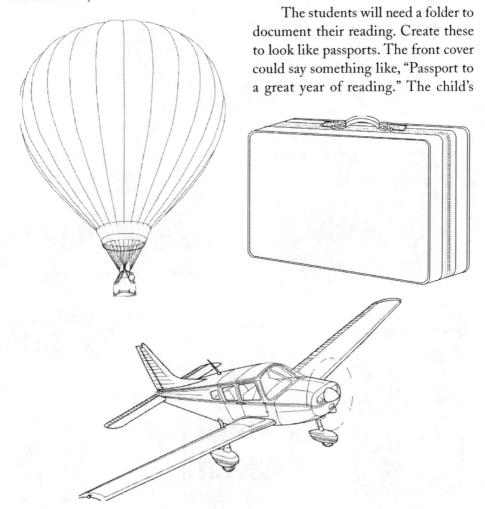

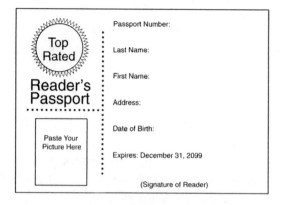

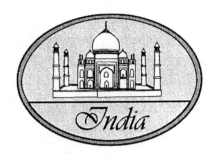

school picture could be included with stickers added for each ten points earned or for each ten books read. Inexpensive stickers can be purchased, or you might even print up your own on the computer. These folders should be laminated to increase their longevity.

Use maps from different parts of the world as backgrounds for bulletin boards. Letters can be cut from old, out-of-date maps. Use globes in every display and call attention to our world as a whole rather than just your little town. Display travel books using old suitcases for display surfaces. You might title them "Welcome to our corner of the world."

Host a festival for students and parents to celebrate the year of reading. This would be an opportunity to show off what everyone has been learning about their classroom country. Foods from the different areas could be served and student art work displayed. Be sure to make a video of this event. Take pictures with a digital camera to add to your school's website.

Create a treasure hunt or trivia game of world locations similar to "Where in the world is Carmen Sandiego?" World maps or copies of *The World Almanac* would be great prizes.

Besides the usual facts the children will learn about countries, it would be a great time to work on map skills. This theme could also be tied to art, music, physical education, math, and basically every subject area. In math, this is an opportunity to work on money skills and the comparison of foreign currency to that of the United States. Use postal stamps and compare the cost, designs, and other features. Is a foreign language taught in your school? Try to include some time for learning a few words in languages such as Spanish, French, German, Japanese, Chinese, or an Arabic language.

The librarian could introduce *Webster's Geographical Dictionary* to students and give them practice in its use. If possible, purchase a new classroom set of atlases for the children to use. Even the smallest children are mesmerized by maps, never mind that they can't read the words. It is important to them to find where they live.

The internet offers unlimited websites to explore:

- http://www.towd.com—This is a tourism website that allows you to type in the name of a state or country you would like information about.

- http://plasma.nationalgeographic.com/mapmachine/plates.html—This is a National Geographic website that allows you to explore the world.

- http://www.capital.com—This has information about countries and their capitals around the world.

- http://www.your-nation.com

- http://www.atlapedia.com

- http://www.geographic.org

- http://www.un.org

- http://www.puzzlemaker.com—This site allows you to make puzzles such as word searches, crossword puzzles and mazes.

Pick out some possible multicultural events to celebrate. The Chinese New Year would be an easy one to incorporate into the curriculum in January or February and Cinco de Mayo would be fun at the end of the school year. Invite storytellers to your school to tell stories from other countries. This is especially important if there isn't much ethnic diversity in your school. Often funding for this is available through area arts councils. Check out all the state resources available.

Your librarian can feature versions of old favorites like the story of Cinderella and other fairy tales to tie them to other cultures. Some of these are: *Yeh-Shen*, The Chinese Cinderella; *The Egyptian Cinderella*; *The Korean Cinderella*; *Raisel's Riddle*, the Jewish Cinderella; *Rough-Face Girl*, an American Indian Cinderella; *Sootface*, an Ojibwa Indian Cinderella; and *Lon Po Po*, the Chinese Little Red Riding Hood.

The children could create travel guides for their classroom country. These could be done on construction paper as a trifold brochure or simply as a poster.

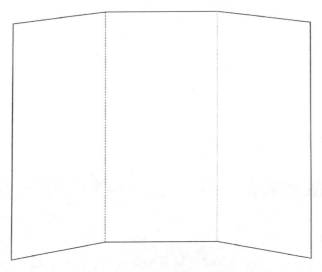

Using the trifold diagram provided fold the paper as shown on the dotted lines.

This will provide six sides to use to give country information, and display photographs or drawings, the flag, etc.

The final design could be photocopied and color added by the students with colored pencils. These could be given out at a special parent function.

When the year is over, you will have encouraged your readers to improve their reading through much practice and the students will, hopefully, understand more about the world they live in.

Read-'em ... Rope-'em

The Old West was indeed wild. The cowboys from the movies and old television shows give us a partial glimpse into the unique world of the American cowboy. This theme could combine the fantasy of the cowboy's life with the reality of the hard work it entailed. Have fun with a theme that features cowboys and rodeos.

Begin the year with a colorful assembly to build enthusiasm for the reading program. Encourage everyone to wear their cowboy garb on that day. Set up the area like a rodeo ring with some barrels and colorful flags. Play some cowboy songs or country music. Have some simple relays for the students, like using stick horses to do some barrel racing. Check with your high school FFA (Future Farmers of America) leader to see which students might be adept at roping. Plan a demonstration during the assembly.

Have your faculty present a silly melodrama. The children will love booing the villain and yelling for the cowboy hero. The sillier, the better. This will help to grab everyone's attention and get the year of reading off to a super start.

Announce the principal's challenge at this assembly. It might be that if the children achieve a school-wide goal of 90 percent or more meeting the required number of points, the principal would dress for a day as a cow, branded of course, or spend the day as a rodeo clown.

To create a reading progress chart, use a large tan or brown tarp for the background. This could simulate the dirt floor of the rodeo ring. Use horses as chart markers. Divide the area with tape, or paint on lines, to designate points or percentages. Use a string of plastic pennants or little flags to add a border to the chart.

To decorate the walls, use horseshoes, cowboy hats, boots, saddles, ropes, a covered wagon, etc. These can be made of paper, or use some of the real items.

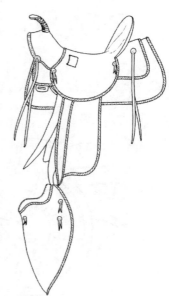

A combination of real and paper would be very effective. Old, worn out cowboy boots could even be used as planters.

Each classroom participating in this reading theme could be considered as a ranch. Branding was developed to indicate the ownership of a specific cow or horse. These brands were quite unique and easily recognizable. Have each class make up a ranch name and design a brand to represent it. This brand should be displayed outside the classroom and could be put on all the horse chart markers for that particular class. See some of the authentic brand designs included in this chapter.

Sponsor a poster contest at the beginning of

the year to create "wanted" posters. These "wanted" posters would be for authors and great books; include your students' favorite authors or award winning books. Provide paper for all who wish to participate and to keep all the entries a standard size. Display them all and choose some to recreate as bookmarks.

Study the major trails to the West. The Oregon Trail is available as a computer game to allow your students to simulate the trip. A trail route might be marked out to the library or the cafeteria.

Use real chunks of wood or cover pieces of carpet tubes to make logs for a campfire. Use red cellophane for the flames. This would create a great area to sit around for a reading class or just a place to sit and read more about cowboys, horses, and the Old West. This would also be a great setting for a music lesson.

Brand Language

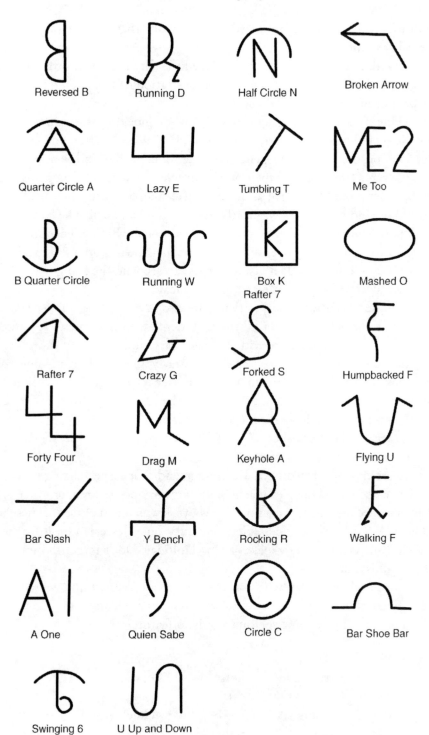

Reversed B   Running D   Half Circle N   Broken Arrow

Quarter Circle A   Lazy E   Tumbling T   Me Too

B Quarter Circle   Running W   Box K Rafter 7   Mashed O

Rafter 7   Crazy G   Forked S   Humpbacked F

Forty Four   Drag M   Keyhole A   Flying U

Bar Slash   Y Bench   Rocking R   Walking F

A One   Quien Sabe   Circle C   Bar Shoe Bar

Swinging 6   U Up and Down

Sing some of the old songs such as: "Clementine," "Home on the Range," "Down in the Valley," "Red River Valley," "Oh, Susanna," "Bury Me Not on the Old Prairie," or "Tumblin' Tumbleweeds." Accompany these with a guitar, or better yet, a harmonica.

Coordinate music class and physical education instruction with some square dancing and line dancing lessons. A demonstration of these could be presented for parents at a PTO or PTA meeting.

Hang up some photographs of old cowboy movie stars. Be sure to include Roy Rogers, the Lone Ranger, Gene Autry, Hopalong Cassidy, and even Zorro. Research on these cowboy legends could be done in the library as a class project. Excerpts from some of their movies or television shows or possibly even an entire movie could be shown as an incentive, complete with popcorn.

Those old movies always clearly marked good and evil. The bad guys wore black hats while the good guys always had white hats. Besides encouraging your students to write some adventure stories of their own, lead a discussion about justice in modern times. Is it always so easy to see who the bad guy is? Why do we have laws? What does it mean to be ethical?

Another incentive opportunity might be to have a hotdogs-and-beans cook-out during the school day for all those students who have met a specific goal. Ask your PTO or PTA to provide the necessary supplies.

Is there a stable or large horse farm near your school? If possible, plan a field trip to allow the students to do some horseback riding. Many children have never seen a horse up close, much less had the opportunity to ride one. Check out the resources available in your community.

Learn to play horseshoes during PE class or at recess. Create some math problems based upon this game.

In art class, study works by Remington and others specializing in "cowboy" art. Create some 3-D papier mâché sculptures of horses, cows, or other figures. Place a cart of biographies nearby of cowboys, lawmen and outlaws. These might include Wyatt Earp, Annie Oakley, Calamity Jane, Jesse James, Billy the Kid, Buffalo Bill, Wild Bill Hickock, or Doc Holliday. Don't forget those tall tales. Pecos Bill is a must!

Check out these websites on the American West: http://www.american west.com, or http://americanhistory.about.com/cs/americanwest.

These might be some spelling words to feature:

lariat	brands	roping
ranch	horse	barrel
chaps	cattle	campfire
spurs	cowboy	chuckwagon
saddle	rodeo	bronco

The Farm

Farms and farm life are the heart of our society. We depend on them for our food and we marvel at their efficiency and the illusion of a slower lifestyle pace. Not as many children today live on farms as in the past, but most children would love to. The animals are so appealing, not to mention the tractors, combines and even the fishing hole. Capitalize on these by featuring aspects of the farm in a theme for this year's reading program.

Does your school district have a local FFA chapter? This Future Farmers of America group could be a great resource for you. You might begin the program with a simple assembly complete with a petting zoo. Children love cows, horses, pigs, sheep and chickens.

Decorations for this theme need not be elaborate. Simply use a few bales of hay or straw with a scarecrow or two—reading of course. A barn could be made out of poster paper or painted on a large sheet of cardboard and hung on the wall. The classroom doors could also be decorated to look like barn doors. Add some wooden kegs, barrels, a few old buckets and lots of baskets.

Look at the painting "American Gothic" by Grant Wood. What about adding a book or magazine to the picture? Add a balloon with catchy words about reading, as though the man or woman was speaking. Talk to the art teacher about more ways to use this painting and how to feature other "farm" art. Some of the cow cartoons in The Far Side series would fit right in also.

To chart reading progress, create a simple field with a large sheet of plain green paper, or use a green tarp. Tape this to the wall or hang it with fishing line. This could become the "north forty" or the "south forty." Use tape to divide the area into sections which represent points or numbers of books and label these new spaces. Tractors would work great as markers to move along to show the child's progress. Photocopy the tractors on white construction paper. Allow the

The "North Forty"

10 20 30 40 50 60 70 80 90 100

children to color them with markers or crayons and to add their names. People seem to have a definite like or dislike for different makes of tractors, just as they seem to have for automobiles. These should be laminated for durability.

Rather than using one large chart for everyone, each class could create their own. They might be individual farms but part of one community. Each child could make a building, such as a barn or house, to put around the edges of this field.

One trip across the field could represent forty points or books read. On the second trip across, change the marker from a tractor to possibly a cow, then a horse, a pig, sheep, chicken, etc. Put up a legend that explains that a tractor represents the first trip across the field, the cow represents the second trip, and so forth. Leave the finished markers on the wall around the field as more decoration and to show that this is definitely a busy farm.

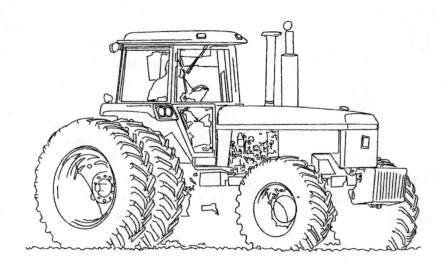

Create some posters or signs with reading-related phrases. Some examples might be:

Ewe Will Love Reading!
Time to Pig Out on Reading!
Read Till the Cows Come Home

A principal's challenge always spurs the children to work hard to reach a school-wide goal. An appropriate one for this theme is for your principal to kiss a pig. If 90 percent of the children achieve their reading goal for the year, the principal would kiss the pig at a closing celebration. Ask around to see if a small pig would be available and then start talking about it to the children to raise the excitement. Be sure to contact your local media to publicize the event.

If field trips are possible, plan one to a local farm. This could be for an entire class or as an incentive for those who have reached a particular goal. Plan some time for a little fishing in the pond.

If a spot is available at your school, plant a garden. Each class could have a particular responsibility in the garden to grow something different. The produce gained could be donated to a food bank in your community or eaten by the children themselves. This whole process would support lessons in nutrition, science and mathematics.

If the garden were six feet wide and ten feet long, how many square feet would it be? Which vegetables require the least amount of water to grow? What are some recipes for zucchini? Why is soil conservation so important? What does erosion mean and what can be done about it?

Check the stock market for an economics lesson in the upper elementary grades. How are crops sold? What does a farmer have to know to make the most money for his crop or livestock? How have farms changed over the years? How are computers used on the farm?

The *Old Farmer's Almanac* is still around and is available online at http://www.almanac.com. Compare this almanac with others found in the library. How do they work and is this old almanac accurate?

Read more about 4-H. Many of your students may be members of this organization. There is a great site on the Internet at: http://www.4-h.org.

Some appropriate spelling words to use might be:

plow	fertilizer	tractor
crops	livestock	elevator
seeds	erosion	bales
cattle	barnyard	fields

Underwater, or Gone Fishing!

Water is a kid magnet! Children love to play in it, whether we're talking about the beach or just a mud puddle. They also are interested in the mysteries under the sea. This theme could be approached from two very different directions. Consider focusing on the marine life under the water and the mystery of underwater treasure, sunken ships, etc. The other direction would be to zero in on the action above the water such as fishing, boating, etc. Or ... just put the two together and go water crazy!

Begin by taping blue plastic around the top of the walls in your classroom or in the main hall of the school. Blue trash bags can be opened up to provide an inexpensive material to simulate water. This plastic doesn't need to come completely to the floor, just use enough to give the quick impression of a water line near the top of the room or hallway. The effect of the blue up high and the fact that it will move a little as people walk by will give you the desired effect.

Use fishing line to hang paper fish and other sea creatures. These could even be made by your students in art class. Coordinate the effort with your school's art teacher. Participation by many people helps to create enthusiasm and ownership of the program.

For a simple chart of reading progress, hang a blue plastic tarp on the wall with strong tape or hang it on the wall with fishing line. Use a colored tape, preferably green, for seaweed to mark off points or percentages earned. Make yellow or orange generic type fish on which you put each child's name. After each fish swims across the entire chart, have the fish swim around the edge of the display to create a great border. Give the child a new, larger size fish to begin again.

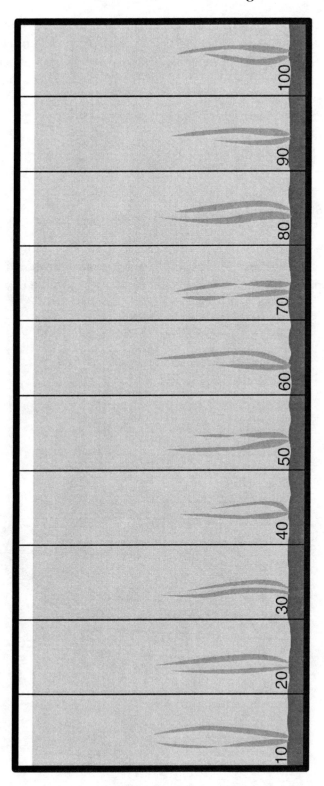

Decorate the area with seashells, nets, and driftwood. Green paper ribbon works well to hang from the ceiling as seaweed. To give the display an even more 3-D look, use inflatable fish water toys like sharks, whales, and octopuses. These could be hung near a display of books with a sign reading, "A Whale of a Tale!"

Inexpensive white paper plates can be made into clams. Using the drawing provided as a guide, fold the plate in half, trim, and round off the edges.

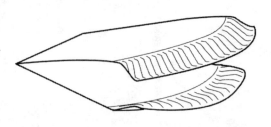

These clams could be used in all types of reading activities or purely for decoration.

Create a display with a treasure chest. Add a sign with a slogan, like: "A good book is a real treasure!" This can be made from a cardboard paper box. Use a strong tape to construct a hinge to secure the lid onto the box.

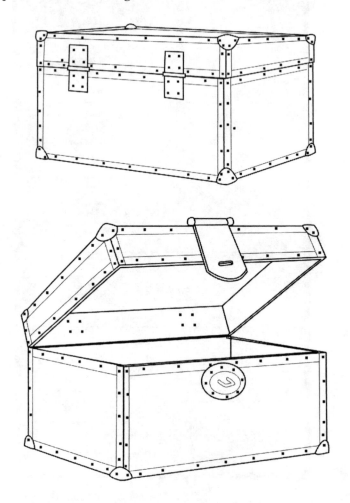

Paint the box a rich brown color. Add strips of paper and fake jewels. Line the inside of the box with some bright red or blue fabric or paper. Fill the treasure chest with books.

A submarine would look great in your overall display. Cut one from a large sheet of cardboard. Paint it in bright colors and name it for your school, such as *S.S. Cole R-5*. Hang it on the wall with fishing line and label it: "We're Diving Into Reading!"

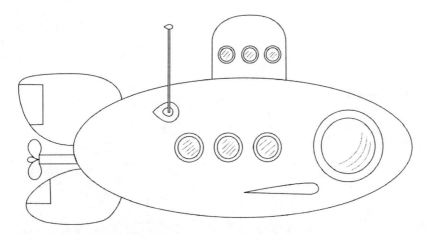

Hang a fishing net near a computer with internet capacity. Add a sign saying, "Try these cool 'net sites." Be sure to hang fish, seahorses, and even turtles in this area to go with the theme. Post these websites for children to explore:

- http://www.enchantedlearning.com/subjects/ocean

- http://www.abc.net.au/oceans/alive.htm

- http://topex-www.jpl.nasa.gov

Use air mattresses as places for the children to sit to read or bring in a real flat-bottomed boat that the children can sit in, or just fill it with books. Nearby, park a cart of books about fish, boats or adventure on the high seas.

To approach this in a different way, focus on the fishing with the slogan "Get Hooked on Reading!" Hang a blue tarp, a blue bed sheet, or a large piece of blue poster paper on the wall. Hang a fishing line for each child over the top of the "water" with a paper clip opened up and tied to the end as the hook. Each time a child earns ten points, a fish could be put on the stringer. If the stringer gets too full, replace the small fish with one really big fish on the line with the appropriate point value listed, like 75. Many of the children will quickly "catch" a bunch of fish.

Sponsor a fishing afternoon at a local pond or lake for all those who have

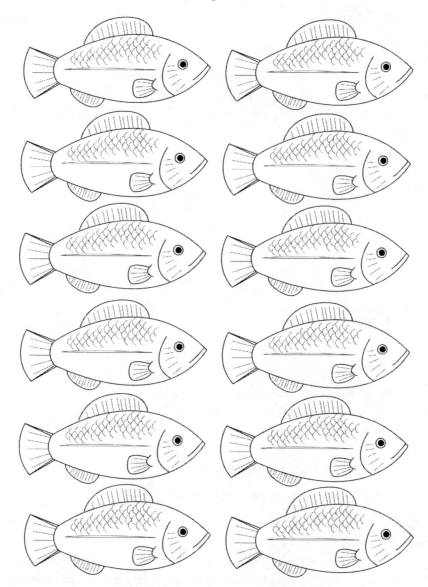

met their reading goal. Weigh and measure all the fish that are caught and do some comparisons for math class.

What is the difference between fresh water and salt water? Where are these types of water located? This would be a great opportunity to work with atlases and to learn more about oceans, rivers and streams.

Fishermen are known for their "whoppers" or highly exaggerated tales of great catches. These could be tied in to a study of tall tales. What a great writing opportunity, too.

Lessons on safety are important at every grade level. This theme would afford the opportunity to discuss all aspects of water safety, whether swimming, boating or just fishing at the edge of the water. If a water patrol officer is available in your area, invite him or her to speak to your students about water safety.

Check out these websites for kids' fishing: http://www.fishingkids.net, or http://www.nebworks.com/kids/angler.htm.

The Rain Forest

Dark and dangerous, yet unbelievably beautiful is a good description of the rain forest. These lush spots of foliage, beautiful birds, and unique animals are disappearing at an alarming rate. This theme might help to call attention to the problem and create a fun year of reading.

This theme could be one that builds on itself as the year progresses. Enlist your art teacher to plan projects that are "jungle" related that can be displayed in the hall to support the theme. This might include paintings of large jungle cats, colorful tissue paper flowers, beautiful butterflies and birds, or exotic plants. The changing hall scenery will help to keep up interest.

Tropical birds photocopied onto white construction paper would make great chart markers. Allow the children to color them with crayons or markers. Colorful feathers could be added along with the child's name. They will look better and last longer if laminated.

Tie a green tarp between two palm trees made from carpet tubes. If your hallway is too narrow for palm trees to sit against the wall, just use fishing line to hang the tarp. Use a colorful tape to mark off the tarp into ten sections. Label these to correspond to point or percentage values. Surround the chart with green paper foliage and bright colorful flowers.

Palm trees can be placed almost anywhere in the building. These are easy to make and are inexpensive. Ask carpet or floor covering stores in your area for their castoff carpet tubes. These can easily be sawed off to the desired length. Use scrap lumber to make a base for each palm tree. Nail three boards together as shown in the illustration.

Nail two boards together to create an X shape. Nail a smaller board at the center of the X so that it can stand up inside the carpet tube. Use two small scraps of wood to balance the X shape.

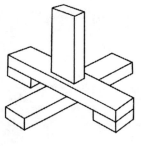

Set the carpet tube down onto the vertical board. Nail or put screws through the tube into the board to secure it in place.

Cut strips of brown mailing paper into fringe and wrap this around the entire tree trunk. Use brown fabric or brown paper to cover the entire base area to make it more attractive.

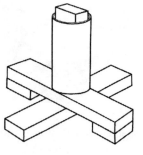

Attaching the leaves to the palm tree can be a challenge. An easy method is to straighten out one wire coat hanger for each leaf you will need. Use pliers to close the sharp end of the wire into a circle so no one will walk into this sharp end. Bend the other end to resemble the illustration. This will allow you to slide the wire onto the top of the tube to attach the leaves.

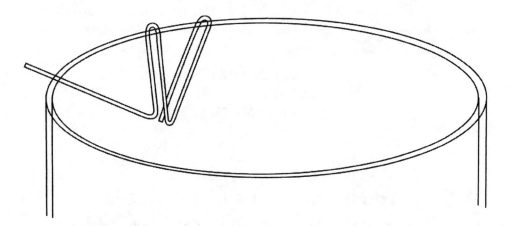

Using a large sheet of green paper, cut an elongated football shape the length of one of your pieces of wire. Cut this shape in a zigzagged pattern to resemble a leaf. Carefully tape the paper to one of the wires prepared according to the previous directions. Use clear tape and use it sparingly because you do not want the tape to be obvious. These leaves can then be bent and shaped to form an interesting tree. Use approximately five to six leaves per tree.

Monkeys and even monkeys reading books could hang from the tops of the palm trees or from vines hanging from the ceiling. Paper ribbon, gift ribbon, or even green yarn would work well for basic vines. Leaves could be added, made from tissue paper, poster paper or construction paper. The leaves can be slightly folded and stapled onto the vines or hot glued into place. Drape the vines around loosely and add some colorful flowers.

As your students read books, have them write the title and author on a green poster paper or construction paper leaf complete with their names. These leaves could be attached to vines and draped throughout the building. This could be a work in progress as the vine continues to grow. The magnitude of the reading effort will be apparent to all.

To help create interest in the rain forest as part of a current events lesson, consider a small fundraising project to help save the rain forests by purchasing an acre or two. The Earth's Birthday Project is an organization that strives to educate children about the earth. Check it out at www.earthsbirthday.org, or at:

Earth's Birthday Project
P.O. Box 1536
Santa Fe, NM 87504-1536
1-800-698-4438

Some possible slogans to consider for this theme might be:

You Toucan Be a Great Reader!
It Can Be a Jungle Out There
Without Good Reading Skills.
Snap Up a Good Book!

Distribute bookmarks often throughout the school year. They are available at a nominal cost from many suppliers but you could make some quite easily

yourself. Choose a rain forest creature and add a catchy slogan. Frogs, snakes, monkeys, alligators, lizards, butterflies, birds or large cats would all work well. Card stock is available in many bright colors and can be run through the copy machine. Use a paper cutter to separate them. For an added touch, punch a hole in the top and insert bright yarn or ribbon. This might be a good opportunity to get your students involved by hosting a bookmark design contest. The winner's design could be produced for everyone in the school.

In the library, create a small free-standing reading hut. This could be just a large cardboard appliance box painted to look like a bamboo hut. Cut out windows and a doorway. Carpet tubes could be taped or wired to the corners of the box to give it strength and to serve as palm trees. Add palm leaves to the tubes and fill the floor of the hut with colorful pillows.

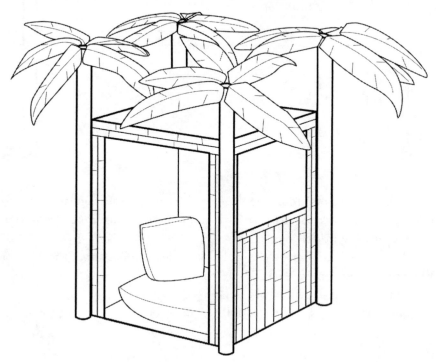

Carpet tubes could be lashed together to create a hut against a wall. Paint the tubes a light yellow color to look like bamboo. Draw in some lines with a permanent brown marker and a brown crayon to give the appearance of bamboo stalks. Use two bases made according to the directions given previously for the palm trees. Stand each of the front poles up on a base and secure in place. Use two tubes for the back poles. Connect the front to back with short pieces of tube cut to fit and then lashed together with rope. It might be wise to screw them together for added strength. Add a piece of cardboard covered with raffia or fringed brown mailing paper for the roof. Trim in vines and flowers.

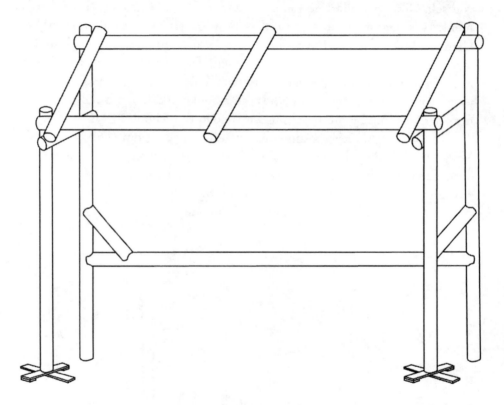

Park a cart of rain forest books near the reading hut. Don't limit it to just books. *Zoobook* magazine, *Ranger Rick,* and *National Geographic World* would be terrific to feature in this area.

Use atlases and other reference books to learn more about the rain forests. Why are they endangered? Why are they so special? How will our world be affected by their disappearance?

There are many websites to visit on this subject, but try out these:

- http://www.pbs.org/tal/costa_rica/rainwalk.html
- http://www.angelfire.com/ar/rainforesttoucan
- http://www.animalsoftherainforest.com
- http://passporttoknowledge.com/rainforest/intro.html

Save Our Planet

Ecology is the science that explains how plants and animals live together and how we are all dependent upon each other. This theme could be used to promote a year of reading in which the students will have an opportunity to understand the importance of each person doing their part and working collectively to save our planet. What an enormous impact this could have on our planet's health.

Divide your school into different habitats. One hall might be the desert (West), one the mountains (North), one under water (East), and one even a jungle or rain forest (South). These areas could be decorated to fit the appropriate habitat. One of the goals for the year would be for each of these areas to share their importance and significance with the rest of the school.

Create a reading progress chart that fits the area. For the desert, use brown mailing paper as a background, divided into point or percentage areas. For chart markers, consider using cactus cut-outs. For the mountains, create a mountain scene on a large sheet of poster paper or paint some mountains on an old tarp. Pine trees or grizzly bears would work well as markers. The underwater and rain forest habitats could be created as outlined in their specific chapters.

Another idea is to pull in camping as a major aspect of the theme. Part of the camping experience is learning to appreciate and understand the great outdoors. Use an outdoor scene for the background of a reading chart or have the children paint a mural on a large sheet of poster paper. Paint in lines to divide the areas into point or percentage designations, or use masking tape. Use drawings of boys and girls as markers.

In the library, set up a small tent to use as a reading area. Set an empty cooler or picnic basket on its side next to the tent to use as a book shelf. Include adventure stories along with books on recycling, the greenhouse phenomenon, conservation and even knot-tying. Throw some sleeping bags around or add a few lawn chairs for comfort.

Decorate with lots of wildlife pictures, butterflies, insects, birds, etc. Use some of them to create some eye-catching posters with catchy slogans like:

Bee a Reader!
Make a Bee-Line to Reading.
Please Don't Bug Me, I'm Reading!
Never Stop Growing. READ!

Have your students begin a school-wide recycling program. Collect aluminum cans and cash them in. Allow the children to choose how to spend the money.

Besides the 3 R's, "reading, writing, and 'rithmetic", there are 4 R's: reduce, reuse, recycle and recover. These could be worked into the theme to promote ecology.

To spur students to keep on reading, offer some incentives like a lock-in at the school. This could even be a read-a-thon. Have a picnic on the playground or a big school-wide barbecue. Go out to a river bank or stream in the area to clean it up, or pick up trash in a nearby park. Whatever the activity, plan to include some time for reading.

Plan a field trip to the closest state or national park. Learn about the history of the park, its special features, conservation measures and other details.

There is much to learn about camping. Some of your students are probably Boy Scouts or Girl Scouts. They will want to share their experiences with the class. Introduce some units on first aid, poisonous plants, or fire safety. Who was Smokey Bear? How did he get his name? Try this website: http://www.campnetamerica.com.

Learn about conservation. Invite a park ranger or state conservation official to speak to your students. Many times conservation education programs include live animals and birds.

Plan a large Earth Day celebration for April. Host a poster contest for your students to promote the environment and, of course, reading. Or, students could design bookmarks instead of posters.

Contact these agencies for more information:

> Department of the Interior
> 1800 D. Street, N.W.
> Washington, DC 20240
>
> Environmental Protection Agency
> Public Information Center
> 401 M Street, S.W.
> Washington, DC 20235
>
> Earth's Birthday Project
> P.O. Box 1536
> Santa Fe, NM 87504-1536
> www.earthsbirthday.org

Take a close look at your school's yard or playground area. Is there a spot that needs to be beautified? Plant a new flower bed or work to clean up and freshen existing flowerbeds. Find an area where wildflowers could be planted. This could become the special project of one class or an entire grade. Contact your state conservation department for suggestions and see if your school might participate in a statewide project or study.

Plant a new tree on the school grounds to honor a great year of reading. Have a special dedication for it to honor Arbor Day.

Some appropriate spelling words to include might be:

garbage	compost	refuse
landfill	decompose	aluminum
waste	recycle	hazardous
ecology	environment	habitat

Once Upon a Time...

Castles, kings, queens, knights ... these are all wonderful parts of a time in history that appeals to most children. Our imaginations conjure up ideas of dragons, chivalry, and Prince Charming. This theme allows the combination of historic facts of the time period and the joy of fairy tales.

To begin the year, stage a colorful assembly. There are groups in many communities who dress in Middle Ages attire and share the culture and stories of that time in history. If one is available near your school, consider inviting them for a demonstration or ask some of your faculty to perform a simple fairy tale–like play. Does anyone on staff juggle or do some magic tricks? Ask your high school students if they might want to be involved. It could even be coordinated with high school literature, drama, or history students as a class project.

This theme could be used school-wide or for a single class or grade. Each class should develop a coat-of-arms which could hang outside the classroom. Each time a child in the class reads a certain number of books, something could be added to the coat of arms. In addition to the coat of arms, large banners could be made from brightly colored poster paper. Research the Middle Ages for heraldry ideas. Some simple designs are included at the end of this chapter.

For a different type of wall chart to keep track of reading progress, build a castle wall of stones. The stones are just pieces of gray construction paper that are splattered with white or black paint to give the illusion of real stone. They should be laminated to cut down on fading if this is a year-long project.

Each time a child reads ten books or earns ten points, have him or her put his or her name on a stone in permanent marker plus the number of points the child has earned—10, 20, 30, etc. Have a teacher or the librarian designated as the wall builder who puts these paper stones "brick-style" on the wall. Be sure to start the wall in a fairly large area. The wall could become quite massive by the end of the year but that could be the goal. This could require quite a bit of maintenance through the year, but it will be spectacular with the addition of some pennants or flags.

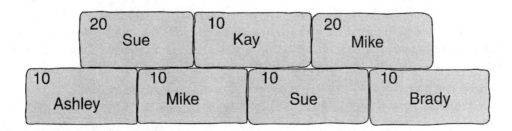

Archways over all the doors could help to give the building a more castle-like look. Use white paper or newsprint drawn into blocks and spattered with black or gray paint to create the arched doorways. Measure a standard doorway and create a pattern. It won't take long to make several arches. Do the spattering on all of them at one time. White lights could be used to outline these doorways to give an even more spectacular look.

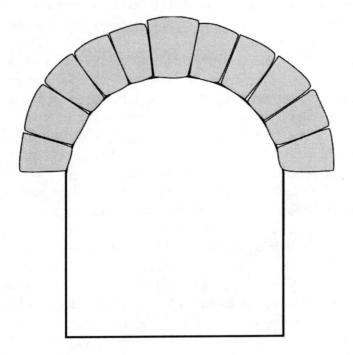

If you desire to go a step further, more defined castle walls could be created in the hall or classroom. It would be a lot of work and take a lot of paper, but whole walls could be made to look like stone. Single stone blocks could be placed around the ceiling in a zig-zag fashion. Towers could be made in the corners of the room or hall. The restrooms could even be labeled "Lords" and "Ladies."

Purple or bright blue plastic tablecloths could be cut into long strips about twelve to eighteen inches wide and draped along the ceiling. Add some silver or gold ribbon to give everything a nice sparkle. Limit the number of colors that you use in your decorating. Blues and purples are good fantasy colors. Go for a well coordinated look with lots of shine. Use a little glitter also, because the desired look is that of a fairy tale castle.

Here are a few phrases to consider:

Find Your Fantasy ... Read!
A Little "Knight" Reading.
Good Knight Reading.

Feature books on fairy tales, King Arthur, castles, the Knights of the Round Table, and even Robin Hood. There are over 1,500 versions of the Cinderella story alone that would fit right in. This would be a great opportunity to compare literature styles using one common theme and to bring more multiculturalism into the curriculum.

Create a dragon out of cardboard boxes. This could become a class project or used simply as an activity for the playground with different groups of children using the same boxes over and over to create new and different dragons.

Dragons appear throughout many cultures. Art class would be a wonderful time to explore these and to even make some using papier mâché. Children don't often have the opportunity to work on 3-D art projects and a project such as this would be beneficial, not to mention fun!

This theme would lend itself well to a unit on etiquette and good manners. Learn about the foods of the time period and coordinate a festival with appropriate food and dancing.

Archery would be a great unit in physical education classes. In conjunction with the music class, simple dances of the time period could be taught.

As a reward for reading progress, have a field day with races in the fashion of a medieval tournament. Include a "dress-up" time for "Lords and Ladies." Children could pretend to be princesses, knights, and other characters from the era. Some may want to ride stick horses. Depending upon the number of points earned or books read, the children could earn particular ranks of nobility. Each time 100 points or some such designated number is reached, the child could move up on the nobility scale with titles such as Earl, Duke, Duchess, Sir Knight, or Prince.

Simple hats could be made in art class such as crowns and tall, pointed princess-style hats. These are made from a piece of poster board shaped into a cone and stapled. A colorful piece of net, tissue paper, light fabric, or ribbon is inserted into the top and allowed to flow freely.

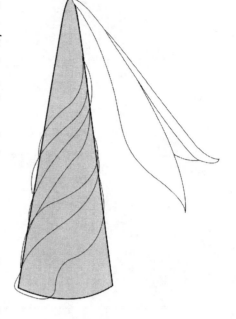

There are many great websites available if you want to visit actual castles. Try one of these with your students:

- www.castles.org

- www.castlesontheweb.com

- www.tower-of-london.com—This is the Tower of London Virtual Tour.

Some spelling words to feature might be:

castle	dragon	steed
medieval	moat	sword
knighthood	drawbridge	armor
chivalry	princess	tournament

Consider making one of these banner designs. Many great reference books are available on this subject to help you as you design additional visuals.

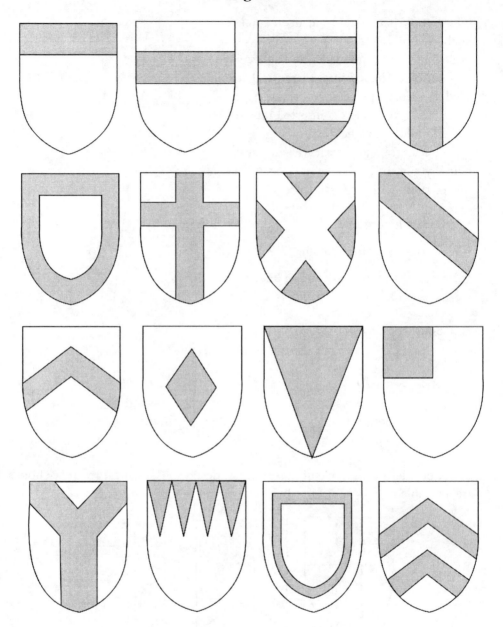

The Olympics

Every four years the world comes together to compete in great athletic contests. The best athletes from all over the globe meet to see who can earn the much coveted gold medal for each sporting event. Use this theme to tie reading to sports and this great world happening. Check out these Internet sites to help you brainstorm for this theme:

- http://www.olympic.org—This is the official website of the Olympic movement.

- http://www.infoplease.com/ipsa/A0114094.htm—This is the best location for comprehensive historical information about the Olympics.

The Olympic rings, one of the official symbols, will be easily recognized by your students and staff. Create a set of these rings to display in the main hallway of the school building. These can be made from inexpensive styrofoam rings. Paint them the appropriate colors or cover them in ribbon or crepe paper and then interlock the rings. Use fishing line to suspend them from the ceiling.

If you need a faster, simpler way to make the rings, just cut out large circles from the appropriate colors of poster board and interlock the circles in the correct color placement. Glue this to a plain, sturdy background.

Put up two large world maps near the olympic rings. Mark the locations of the summer game sites through history on one map and the winter sites on the other. It is a special honor for a city to be chosen to host the event. This would be a great visual aid for a geography lesson. Organize a geography bee for your school this year.

The World Almanac is a great tool to use to see flags from all over the world. Create some from construction paper or print some with your computer printer. These flags could be hung from the ceiling or put on the wall side by side to create an appropriate border in the hallway.

Each class could make their own flag, which would make some statement about reading. Hang these in a prominent location as a symbol of school and reading pride. Have an opening and a closing assembly similar to the ceremonies of the real Olympics. These class flags would add to the excitement of the moment. When the children carry them into the assembly, just as the flags of participating countries are proudly carried into the olympics. Retire the class flags at the closing assembly.

A wall chart will be needed to show the children's reading progress. This could be done as a race track, and the easiest would be a straight, horizontal track. Use painter's tape directly on the wall to make the point or percentage designations. Label each and be sure to make a fairly large sign that signifies the finish line. Add a cheering section to the top of the track with smiley, encouraging faces or just use smiley stickers. Some colorful pennants would look cool, also.

A tennis shoe would be a great chart marker. A pattern is included in this chapter. These could be photocopied onto any color of construction paper or cardstock. The children could personalize their tennis shoes with crayons or markers. Laminate these if possible. Move the tennis shoe along as points are earned, books are read or the specific percentages are earned.

Enlarge the tennis shoe design and copy it on white paper. Use these to provide your students with a place to name their favorite book and write a book review. These can be colored with crayons or markers. Display these heel-to-toe around the halls. This could become a massive display as the year progresses and a great visual tool to show just how many great books your students are reading.

These are some good slogans to use for this theme. Consider one or more of these:

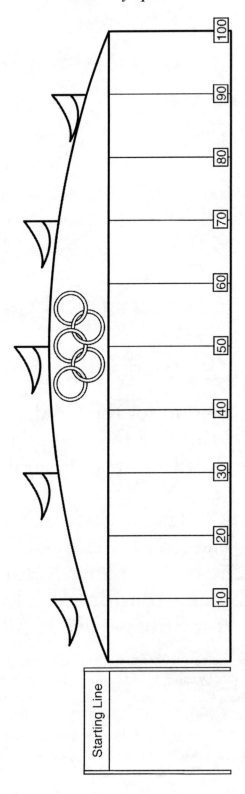

Go for the Gold!
Reading for the Gold!
Readers Break Records
Ready ... Set ... Read!
Read to Succeed!
The Best Is Yet to Come!
Catch Up on Your Reading!
Exercise Your Brain ... Read!
Finish the Year Strong. Give It All You've Got!

Another important symbol of the Olympics is the torch. Create a torch for your reading olympics by using an old bucket, a box fan, crepe paper, cellophane, and a cardboard box. Cut the bottom out of the bucket, then cut a hole in the cardboard box and insert the bucket. Cut the bottom out of the cardboard box. Paint the bucket and box with a white or cream colored paint. Splatter these with black and gray paint to give it a stone appearance. Lay the fan on its back to blow the air upward. Set the bucket and box over the top of the fan. Strips of red and orange crepe paper and cellophane should be attached to the inside of the bucket. The fan will blow these upward to resemble flames and they will even give a slight crackling sound. Set this torch on a small table or some type of pedestal. A vine of leaves could be wrapped around it or some other means of decoration added.

Research the ancient Greeks and the original Olympic games. Research major occurrences at the games, such as the one in which Jesse Owens participated. Discuss the importance and significance of the Olympics. What does good sportsmanship mean? Compare the summer and the winter games. How are they alike and different?

For a math activity, create some problems related to some of the events. If a marathon race is 26 miles and 385 yards long, how many feet is that? How many inches are in a marathon? Create bar graphs of the number of medals won by different countries.

During the closing assembly, award medals to all students who achieved their reading goal for the year. Inexpensive medals are available from most educational supply distributors.

Outer Space

Going where no man has gone before excites our imagination. We are drawn to movies and shows such as *Star Wars*, *Star Trek*, and *Apollo 13*. Space travel has become a reality for a few, but the majority of us just marvel at the idea of it all. This theme could really rocket your students into a great year of reading.

How about these slogans:

3–2–1—Blast Off ... READ!
Rocket Into Reading
Star Readers
Take Off with a Good Book!

There are several ways to create a chart to measure reading progress. For the basic background, use a large sheet of heavy black plastic which you secure to the wall with tape or hang like a tarp. Black paper would work, but it will not look as good once markers are moved across it several times. The finish of the paper will not last long. Create an orange or bright yellow-orange sunburst shape from laminated construction paper to serve as the sun. Position it in the lower left area of the black plastic. This would serve as a large area for everyone to begin. A sign there could say, "We're red-hot readers!" Paint lines or use masking tape to mark off the area for point or percentage designations. Add a planet to each point line, appropriately labeled. Foil silver stars could be added for a little pizazz.

Simple rocket ships could serve as markers. Photocopy these onto gray or light blue construction paper and then laminate them. Use a permanent marker

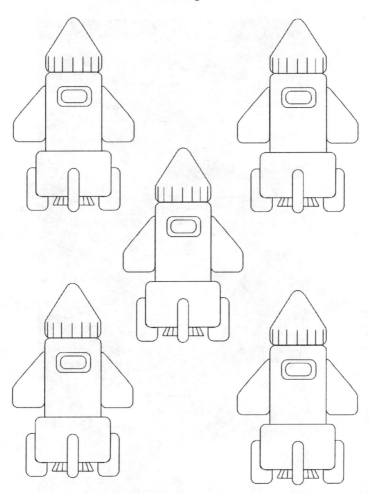

to add the child's name. Each time a trip is made across the solar system or 100 points is earned, a star could be added to the ship.

Another way to make the chart would be to use the black plastic and the sun as before, but eliminate the dividing lines. Make the nine planets from construction paper and divide each into ten segments. The rocket would orbit the planet until the necessary points were earned and then move to the next planet. After 100 points are earned, the ship could take a comet ride back to the sun to begin again.

Use star shapes cut from foil paper and position them in the arrangement of common constellations such as the Big Dipper or Orion's Belt. Label these. They could even be done in fluorescent paint on a black background. Liberally hang white Christmas lights around the doorways and in the hall. This will also give the illusion of many stars.

Cut large stars from silver foil paper or metallic poster board. Whenever a child reaches 100 points or a particular goal, write his or her name on a star.

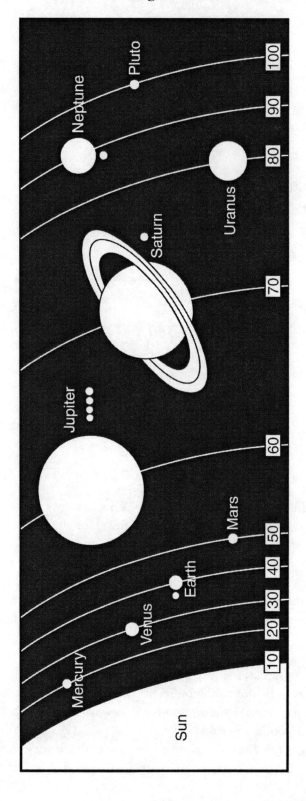

Hang the stars from the hallway ceiling. This will help everyone to see how close the school is to meeting the goal for the year. Hopefully your principal would be willing to do something pretty out-of-this-world if, for instance, 90 percent of the students reach their goal by the end of the year. He or she could be dressed as an alien for a day, sit on the roof for the day in his or her pajamas, etc. The sillier the challenge, the better.

Study of the planets and the stars is a unit in almost every grade's science class. This would be an opportunity to tie science and reading together. Since there are nine planets and generally nine months of school, feature one planet a month and learn as much as possible about that planet. Create math problems relating to that planet, spelling words, or other lessons. Mars, in particular, would be fun to do because you could bring in some old science fiction movies that contain Martians, trips to the planet, or other science fiction. There is even an old movie about Martians coming to capture Santa Claus and take him back to their planet.

In the library, feature books on the planets and all about NASA. There might even be someone in your community with NASA-related experience, or contact NASA and invite someone to visit your school. Work to set up a link via satellite with one of the space centers.

To create an interesting spot for reading in the library or a classroom, use a cardboard appliance box to construct a rocket ship. Add some cardboard triangular pieces as tail fins. Paint the box or use aluminum foil to cover it, adding some glitter or stickers. Fill the floor area with soft, comfortable pillows and park a cart of space-related books nearby. These might include biographies of Galileo, Copernicus, John Glenn, or Sally Ride.

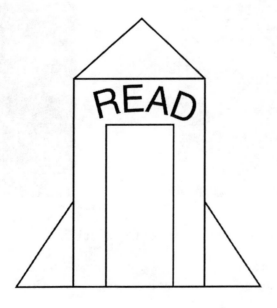

The Internet is a fountain of information on space and space travel. These sites will get your research started:

- http://www.nasa.gov
- http://www.astronomy.com
- http://www.spacestation.com
- http://quest.arc.nasa.gov
- http://www.seo
- http://www.governmentguide.com/research_and_education/science/space
- http://www.meteorcrater.com

Bookmarks are always popular with children. Sponsor a contest to get possible designs. The prize is having your design chosen for the bookmark. It doesn't hurt to give bookmarks out several times during the year.

Some possible spelling words to feature might be:

| rocket | gravity | meteor |
| universe | atmosphere | planet |

astronomy	asteroid	constellation
space	comet	lunar

To bring more multiculturalism to the curriculum, research legends of the stars and the heavens. Many Native American legends are available on cassette and in books. Compare the stories of different tribes and learn how the stars were placed in the sky, how certain constellations received their names, or why some animals have no stars named for them. A Native American living in your area might come to share these with your students. Other cultures have similar legends and, with just a little research on your part, you just might locate someone in your community to come to your school.

If you choose this theme to use school-wide, consider dividing up the building, giving different hallways the names of planets. If it is a long walk to the cafeteria, perhaps it could be on Pluto. A sign could be placed in the foyer of the school with a phrase like:

Welcome to Our Universe!
The Adventure Begins Here!

Community Helpers

No place is more special to your students than your own community. This could be a big city, small town, rural community, or neighborhood. Base your reading theme this year on your own city or town and the many untapped resources just waiting for you.

Create a reading wall chart that looks much like a very large Monopoly board. This board game has been redone for national parks, state information, pro-sports, and many other themes, so why not create one of your own?

Use a large tarp of any solid color as the background for this wall chart. Use masking tape or some cool color of plastic tape, or even paint on the lines to divide up the area. See the design on the next page as a suggestion. Put a picture of your school in the center since your students are the center of this program. If you have extra school pictures of your students, put them side by side to create a border around the chart.

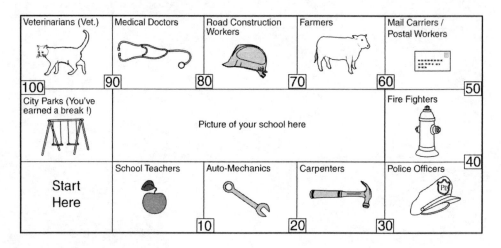

Add a small sign in each space with a symbol for the business and the name of that specific business in your community. If there are many convenience stores, for example, and you don't want to leave out a local taxpayer, just list the type of business rather than a specific business name.

For chart markers to move around the game board, consider your school mascot, a boy or girl, or just a smiley face. Add the child's name.

Much emphasis is given to career development in our schools. Host a career fair coordinating this event with your school counselor. Invite people from your community to speak to the children about their occupations. This might include the education required, technology used on the job, the income possibilities, the pros and cons of the job, etc. Some occupations to feature could be:

fireman
policeman (especially the DARE
  officer)
baker
bus driver
mailman
veterinarian
doctor
dentist

nurse
mechanic
barber or beautician
artist
sales manager (cars, clothing)
carpenter
road construction
farmer

Each month, have some special event that relates to the areas on the chart board. The goal is for your students to learn more about their community—past and present—as they also improve their reading skills. Invite community leaders to come in and read their favorite books to the children and to tell stories of life ten, twenty, or thirty years ago. This would be a fantastic opportunity to organize a volunteer program utilizing senior adults. We need more community participation, and tying that to reading is a plus for everyone. Children would love to have someone just listen to them read and to give them a little love and praise.

For a writing project that's also a history lesson, pair up a student with a World War II veteran, Korean War veteran, Vietnam War vet, or Desert Storm vet in your community. The student could interview the veteran, write a report or even prepare a PowerPoint presentation. These could be put on the school website for all of the community to enjoy. New friendships will be created and the children will hear firsthand what these veterans experienced. Don't forget about all those who waited for them at home. Those would be great interviews, too.

Calendar

Consider choosing a calendar theme for this year's reading program. The best thing about this theme is that there won't be time for you or your students to become bored. It is also great because it provides an opportunity for each student to have a fresh start each month. If the student is not particularly successful one month, there is hope for the next month with a different emphasis.

"Under the Big Top" might be a grand way to begin the year. The lure of the circus just might be what you need to draw in those hesitant readers. Use slogans such as:

Reading ... the Greatest Show on Earth! We're Big on Reading!

Decorate the hallways with strings of colored plastic flags or pennants similar to those used at car dealerships. Colored Christmas tree lights would look very dramatic and festive strung around the classroom doorways. Drape red ribbon or crepe paper across the ceiling to simulate a circus tent. Start in the middle of the ceiling and work outward like the spokes on a wheel.

Use lots of clowns and balloons to decorate. Encourage everyone to come dressed as a clown on one particular day to kickoff the theme. Stage a talent show with your principal as the ring master. Serve peanuts, popcorn, snow cones or cotton candy for the event.

Someone on your faculty just might have some circus posters that they would be willing to share for the month. Display images of elephants, dazzling horses, trapeze artists and circus wagons. In a corner out of the way, hang a pretend trapeze complete with a stuffed animal, like a monkey, hanging on while reading.

You won't want to create a wall chart over and over each month for a new theme emphasis. Each child might instead have a calendar page for each school month. On a bulletin board in each classroom or on a large sheet of poster paper displayed in the hall, put up a calendar page for each student. Use tape or in some way attach this to be replaced with a new one next month. Take the old sheets down and have the children keep them in a reading folder. The children can use a pencil, pen or marker to list the number of points earned or books read on each day. Tally up the total at the end of the month. If resources allow, give small incentives based upon achievement.

Plan a special event for each month that only those who have met the reading goal can participate in or attend. Make sure that all the children understand the program and that their hard work at reading determines their participation in special events. Be sure the next big event is widely publicized. It would be wise to send a note home to parents which explains the plan for the year and encourages parents to participate. Schools need more parent involvement.

Form a committee of faculty, staff and parents to plan the year's events at the beginning of the program. This will allow event adequate time to make all the preparations for each event and will eliminate the last minute hysteria that goes with poor planning. Some events can be simple and on a small scale, but plan at least one really big, exciting event for the year. Save something terrific for the end of the year that will be worth working for. Be sure to notify the local newspapers and television stations so your events will receive news coverage.

Whatever you choose as the month's event, plan some simple decorations to help to promote it. A display of real items is easiest and you might choose a central location such as the library to set up a new display each month. Streamers are inexpensive and balloons are attention-getting. The decorating task might be given to different grades or classes each month to get the children involved in the process. Try to tie everything to reading in some way, since that is the whole reason for the effort.

It isn't necessary to celebrate nationally recognized holidays, as most of those will be given attention in the classroom anyway. Make up some silly new holidays or plan fun events.

Here is a list of some possible activities:

• Visit an apple orchard or pumpkin farm.

• Go fishing at a local pond or lake.

• Yabadabadoo … have a Flintstones dress-up day!

• Do a community service project such as picking up trash or raking leaves for some elderly person near the school.

- Celebrate cowboy day complete with a hayride and a pretend rodeo. Make a simple cowboy-style movie.

- Have a skating party—roller skates or ice skates depending upon your location.

- Plan a read-a-thon at the school—possibly for the entire night.

- Celebrate Elvis' birthday with a '50s sockhop.

- Have pajama day allowing the students and teachers to wear their pajamas and house slippers. Have everyone bring their pillows and favorite munchies and just read for the day.

- Celebrate the Chinese New Year complete with a dragon, a parade and yummy food.

- In the middle of winter have a blah-buster party. Everyone could come in their beach clothes (no swimming suits) and play beach ball volleyball, hula hoop, etc. Bring in lawn chairs, and beach towels, and put up palm trees.

- Go to a pig farm or a dairy farm.

- Host a movie star day. Each person chooses a movie star to become for the day. Make a school movie or do some interviews. Show a movie and serve popcorn.

- Plan a big Earth Day celebration. Plant a tree at the school and dedicate it to all the school's great readers. Possibly plant a tree for each child who has achieved a particular number of points or some specific designation.

- Spend the afternoon flying kites.

- Have a faculty-student baseball game complete with popcorn or snow cones for the fans.

- Have a school carnival and include a dunk tank.

- Give an extra 60 minute recess.

- Have a silly hat day.

- Have a craft afternoon—learn to tie-dye, make sculptures from found materials, make nature crafts, or other creative items.

- Go bowling.

- Have a petting zoo visit the school.

- Have a field day with relays, races, kickball games, etc.

- Have a pioneer day with old-timey crafts, food and games.

- Celebrate a day such as your state's birthday with everyone dressing up as a famous person from your state. Have a pageant or fashion parade with activities based on facets of your particular state.

- Go on a nature walk. This could be on the school grounds or at a nearby state or national park.

- Allow some students to assume the role of teacher, principal, coach, librarian, cook, custodian, secretary, or other school personnel. They make great assistants.

- Invite a storyteller to visit the school and tell stories to the children.

- Host a hobby day with a hobby fair in which the children can bring in examples of their hobbies.

- Make ice cream sundaes.

- Have an afternoon of cool science projects and experiments.

- Invite in local celebrities, including local television personalities.

- Celebrate Mickey Mouse's birthday with cake, ice cream and, of course, a movie.

- Spend an afternoon putting together packages of snacks, personal items, or other small gifts for our servicemen and women. Have the children write letters to go with the treats. Check to see who from your area might be serving overseas and concentrate on them.

- Paint the playground equipment and clean up the school grounds. Plant flowers and give the area a new look.

There are really no limits to this reading promotion. Be creative and choose activities that will be exciting to *your* students—you know them better than anyone. The important thing to remember is that all the activities should be tied to reading. Use the library as your main resource to prepare the children for the chosen event. Your librarian will love being an important player in all the action.

Under Construction

Do you need a short-term theme that would appeal to your hard-to-moti-vate readers? Consider a construction theme. This would be great for a single classroom or it could be expanded school-wide. Your school is a "construction site" where great readers are being built.

Start with a catchy slogan:

We're Under Construction.
Readers at Work.
Reading ... a Building Block to Your Future.
This Is a Construction Site!

Your principal or reading teacher could serve as the site foreman. Require hard hats for your management team along with overalls, jeans or other basic work clothes on the opening day.

Decorate the walls with paper tools, gloves, shovels, and other work implements. Real tools could be used in a display case along with some great books. Use copies of schematic drawings or copies of actual blueprints as backgrounds for bulletin boards or to decorate the walls. Include some signs like:

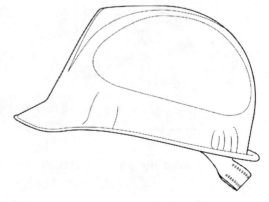

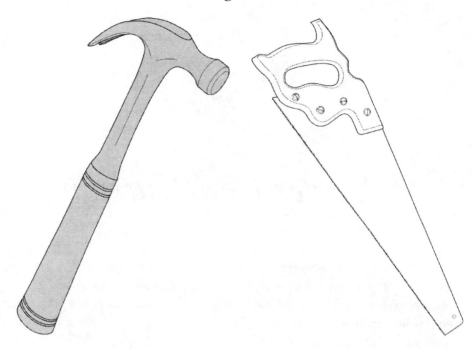

Quiet ... Reading Zone.
Only Readers Allowed in This Area.

To chart reading progress, use bricks as markers. Make these bricks from laminated red construction paper. Every time a child earns ten points or reads a certain number of books, write his or her name on a brick in permanent marker. Build a wall one brick at a time. This could become a massive display and might require one person to be responsible for placing the bricks and for maintenance.

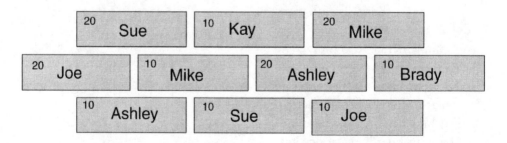

As part of the program kickoff, invite a local contractor, possibly a school parent, to bring in a large piece of equipment such as a bulldozer. The children will enjoy seeing big machines like a dump truck or even a road grader.

Organize a group of students to build something on the playground. Cardboard boxes would work or, if a quantity of sand is available, create a large sand castle. The process of building is much more important than the product.

Check with your PTO or PTA parents to see who might be willing to donate wood or wood scraps for a class to build something. Parents could also be involved in teaching the children how to properly handle tools. Check with your school district's Industrial Technology or "shop" teachers to see if a demonstration of proper safety could be given to your students by some high school students.

Also with parent involvement in mind, ask your PTO or PTA to consider purchasing a new piece of playground equipment. Organize a work day to install it or just to give the old equipment a bright, new coat of paint. Some general cleanup jobs around the school could be done in an afternoon.

This sounds like a really hands-on theme, but you can tie it all back to reading with books on big trucks, construction tools, and even simple machines like levers, wedges, inclined planes, etc. Books on bridges, buildings, and other forms of architecture would be appropriate.

Craftsmen must always measure and then check the measurements again for accuracy. Feature lessons using rulers, yardsticks, and tape measures. Measure the entire building, if possible, as a math activity. How many inches long is your classroom?

Try this great website: http://www.lego.com.

Spelling words to feature might be:

hammer	blueprint	equipment
bulldozer	architect	incline
construction	contractor	measurement
accuracy	foreman	materials

The Ice Cream Parlor

I scream, you scream, we all scream for ice cream! We all love the stuff and it could be a really fun and yummy incentive for reading. This theme might be tough to maintain for a year, so consider it for only a month or two. This would be lighthearted and fun for everyone and a perfect theme for a summer reading program.

Some possible slogans might be:

Give Yourself a Treat … Read!
Reading Is So Cool!
A Good Book Is a Sweet Treat!

Reading progress could be shown on a wall chart in several different ways. As in other themes, each child could have a marker to move along point or percentage designations which have been marked on some type of background, such as a tablecloth. For the ice cream theme, it could begin with an empty dish for each child. At each marker point, something could be added to the dish. For example: at 10 points or 10 percent, add a scoop of ice cream, at 20 points or 20 percent add the syrup, at 30 points or 30 percent add some sprinkles, at 40 points or 40 percent add whipped cream, at 50 points or 50 percent add some nuts, at 60 points or 60 percent add a cherry and so forth. After the ice cream is added, the rest could be added with colored markers.

Another possibility would be to use a bowl of ice cream and move this all the way across the chart. After the first goal is met, add syrup or some type of topping for the next trip across. This could be done with permanent markers or items could be glued on. As some children earn many points, this sundae could

be quite yummy looking by the end of the year. Glue could be spread on the marker and real sprinkles added like glitter.

For a third idea, attach a large plastic tablecloth to the wall. Using velcro, fasten a dish marker in place on the tablecloth for each child. Instead of moving the marker, each time ten points are earned, the child could add something to the dish. The marker could be taken down and each new ingredient could be glued on or drawn on. Keep adding more scoops of ice cream and toppings.

At the end of the time period, have an ice cream party. Each child could recreate the sundae that he or she had created on the wall. Ask your PTA, PTO or parents to supply the ingredients for these sweet treats.

A principal's challenge always encourages the children to press on. For an off-the-wall challenge, allow the students to make your principal into an ice cream sundae. Use a plastic swimming pool for the bowl and have your principal sit in it as the ice cream. Be sure he or she wears goggles to protect the eyes.

Put various toppings in small condiment cups. Allow those students who have reached their goal to pour a topping over the principal's head. Top off the sundae with spray whipped cream. A nice shower will clean your principal up again, but the children will always remember the event!

For a math activity, make ice cream using a hand-cranked freezer. Have the students follow a recipe to mix up the ingredients. How much of each ingredient would have to be used to double the recipe?

For a nutrition lesson, discuss good eating habits. What is the difference between ice cream and ice milk? What is the importance of calcium in our diet? Check out these ice cream websites:

• http://www.ocbtracker.com/ladypixel/icecrem.html—Ice cream recipes from famous ice cream vendors.

• http://aol.drspock.com/article/0,1510,59411+++,00.html—Thirteen fun facts about ice cream.

If ice cream isn't your thing, consider a picnic as the theme. Use a large plastic tablecloth on the wall for the background of the wall chart. The marker could be a sandwich in the making. Begin with a paper plate; then, add bread, mustard or mayo, cheese, ham, lettuce, pickles, etc. as points are earned. A hot-dog with chili and cheese or relish would work well, too. Celebrate the finale with a sandwich-making party.

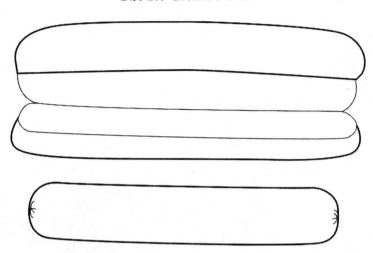

Use ants around the edges of the wall chart and on the walls because we always have them with us at picnics. Use other summertime symbols like slices of watermelon, suns, sunglasses, cool drinks, a picnic basket, or others from your own creativity.

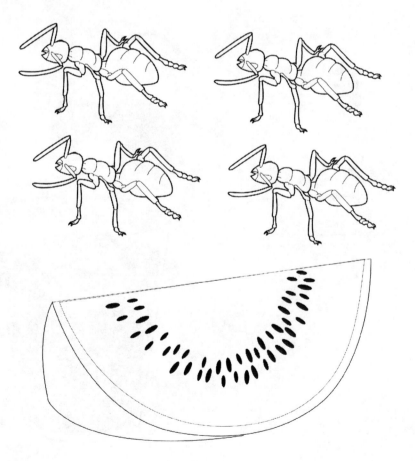

For a display space to showcase some great books, use a picnic table festively decorated. Consider using an empty cooler or picnic basket sitting open on its side for a temporary bookshelf. Bring in some lawn chairs or use some brightly colored beach towels for the children to sit on and read.

Whichever way you go with this theme, create some bookmarks to give to the children. These are great to distribute a week or two into the program to spur those reluctant readers along. Bookmarks cost next to nothing to make and children seem to love to get a new one. You might provide the materials and let them create one of their own design.

Pizza Pizazz

Mama Mia ... What Wonderful Readers!

Pizza is a staple of the American diet. There are very few children who dislike it and they all seem to have a favorite, whether it's pepperoni, sausage or even a supreme. Capitalize on this love of pizza by featuring it as your reading program theme. This theme works well for a single classroom but could also be stretched school-wide. It might be difficult to maintain enthusiasm for an entire school year, but it could be very effective for a month or two.

Create your own classroom pizza parlor by starting at the hall door. Make an awning that hangs over the entry. A simple way to do this is to use an inexpensive plastic tablecloth. Red would be a great color and would be very attention-getting. Tape one side of the table cloth to the wall above the door. Be generous with the tape.

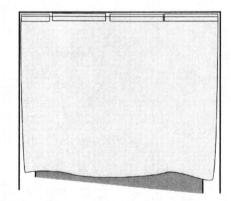

Use a dowel rod the width you would like this awning to be. Measure the amount of overhang you would like for the awning; scalloping the edge is optional. Tape the tablecloth to the dowel rod on the underside to create a casing. Attach a piece of fishing line to each end of the dowel rod. Tape the fishing line in place on the dowel rod to keep it from slipping off.

Attach a utility hook or a large paperclip (opened up) to the ceiling band

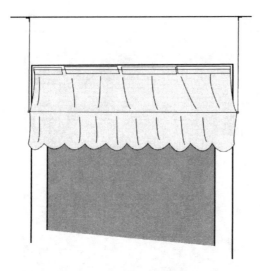

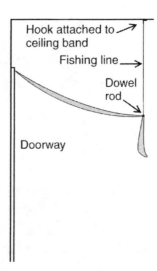

on either side of the awning. Tie one piece of fishing line to one clip and (Insert side view of awning) then do the same with the other. You are creating a trapeze-like awning. Add a sign with the teacher's name on it such as "Mrs. Johnson's Pizza Parlor."

Use a red and white checked tablecloth as the background of a reading chart. This can be taped to the wall or hung as a tarp with fishing line. Begin with an empty paper plate for each child. Attach a piece of Velcro to the back of the plate and a corresponding piece on the tablecloth. Place a small sign under each plate that says something like, "This is Charlie's pizza!"

Have tan construction paper cut into slightly smaller circles than the paper plate. Divide these circles into ten pizza slices. Each time ten points or ten books are read, add a slice of pizza to the plate. The child could decorate each slice using markers, crayons, or small scraps of paper to add sauce, cheese, pepperoni, or other toppings, and it could be glued in place on the paper plate. After a full pizza is created, set it aside as a decoration and begin a new plate for the student. A "2nd" could be added to the child's sign.

Red and white checked tablecloths would work well to decorate other areas of the building as well as making good backgrounds for bulletin boards. Add some aprons and paper chef hats to the decor.

At the end of the reading program, host a pizza party. The students could possibly make the pizzas themselves with the help of the cafeteria workers, or just order in. Your PTO or PTA might supply the ingredients or the pizzas.

Many local pizza restaurants offer free pizza coupons for schools to use as awards or incentives. Check restaurants in your area and beg for some for your great readers.

This theme will allow you to teach nutrition lessons. Can pizza be nutritious? Where did pizza originate? Research some of the most popular foods in

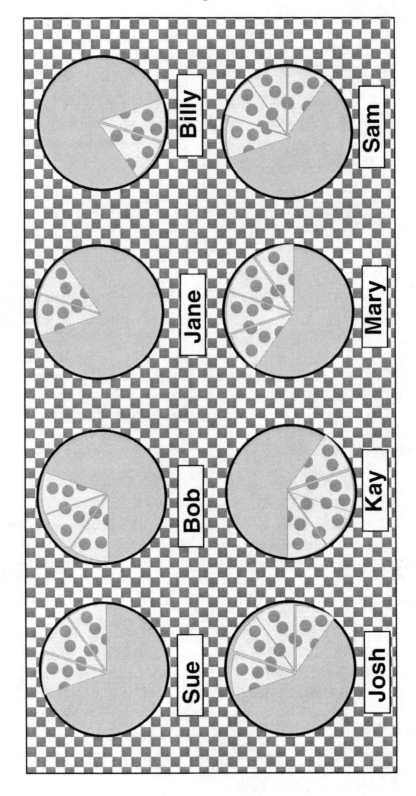

the United States. How many calories are in a slice of cheese pizza? How about a fruit pizza?

Use pizzas to teach fractions or make graphs showing the class favorite. How can the recipe for thick crust pizza be doubled?

Some possible spelling words might be:

sauce	pepperoni	bacon
topping	sausage	crust
cheese	pepper	wedge
mozzarella	onion	slice

Index

111